DISCERNMENT
Seeking God
In Every Situation

DISCERNMENT
Seeking God
In Every Situation

Rev. Chris Aridas

Resurrection Press
An Imprint of
CATHOLIC BOOK PUBLISHING CORP.
Totowa • New Jersey

Revised edition published in March, 2004 by Resurrection Press, Catholic Book Publishing Corporation.

ISBN 978-1-878718-88-4

Library of Congress Catalog Number: 2003115775

Photo and cover design by John Murello

Printed in the United States of America

3 4 5 6 7 8 9

Dedication

I dedicate this book to my spiritual director, Sr. Ann Marino, RSHM, whose gentle guidance and constant encouragement have helped me maintain my bearings and recognize God's Spirit as I journey to the Kingdom.

Acknowledgments

My sincerest thanks to Emilie Cerar, my editor, whose invitation to rework this manuscript was an answered prayer. In addition, I am grateful to Beth DeNapoli who took care of all the e-mail correspondence, making sure that the manuscript went safely from disk to text, and John Murello, my long time Gospel co-worker, who designed the cover. Finally, I want to thank all those who repeatedly asked to have this manuscript revised. Their encouragement and repeated requests helped bring this project to its conclusion.

Contents

Introduction

Blessed be the God and Father of our Lord Jesus Christ,
who has blessed us with all the spiritual blessings of heaven
  in Christ.
Thus he chose us in Christ before the world was made
to be holy and faultless before him in love,
marking us out for himself beforehand, to be adopted sons
  [and daughters],
through Jesus Christ.
Such was his purpose and good pleasure,
to the praise of the glory of his grace,
his free gift to us in the Beloved,
in whom, through his blood, we gain our freedom, the for-
  giveness of our sins.
Such is the richness of the grace
which he has showered on us
in all wisdom and insight.
He has let us know the mystery of his purpose,
according to his good pleasure which he determined before-
  hand in Christ,
for him to act upon when the times had run their course:
that he would bring everything together under Christ, as
  head,
everything in the heavens and everything on earth.
And it is in him that we have received our heritage,
marked out beforehand as we were,
under the plan of the One who guides all things

as he decides by his own will,
chosen to be,
for the praise of his glory,
the people who would put their hopes in Christ before he
   came.
Now you too, in him,
have heard the message of the truth and the gospel of your
   salvation,
and having put your trust in it
you have been stamped with the seal of the Holy Spirit of the
   Promise,
who is the pledge of our inheritance,
for the freedom of the people whom God has taken for his own,
for the praise of his glory.   Eph 1:3-14

Discernment is a fascinating subject. It broadens our horizon, challenges our faith, raises our hopes, seeks to allay our fears. We all want to know "how to discern," how to know God's will. Undoubtedly, you are hoping that this book might give you the answer—or at least provide a reasonable outline: which prayer to say, when to say it, and how to understand the answer.

Such a hope, however, will lead to disappointment, for that is not where *Discernment: Seeking God in Every Situation* is going to take you. In reality, there is no magic prayer, no special time, no favored sign or gesture that reveals God's will for us—except Jesus. Jesus is the Father's will for us. Jesus, the Word of the Father spoken in time through the sign of a Virgin. He is the Father's will for us in every situation. Should you decide to continue, knowing that this will be the direction taken, begin by relaxing. Sit back; hum a hymn; quietly praise and thank the Father for making it as simple as a Word. Say that Word: "Jesus." Remember: it is through Jesus that we are held in the arms of a loving Father, a Father who cares for us, loves us, and forgives us.

Begin by praying a psalm to relax you. Two short ones are printed below. Pray one or the other, slowly, peacefully. Savor the words, the promises given, the hopes instilled.

> *I rely, my whole being relies,*
> *   Yahweh, on your promise.*
> *My whole being hopes in the Lord,*
> *   more than watchmen for daybreak:*
> *more than watchmen for daybreak*
> *   let Israel hope in Yahweh.*   Ps 130:5-7

> *Yahweh, my heart is not haughty,*
> *   I do not set my sights too high.*
> *I have taken no part in great affairs,*
> *   in wonders beyond my scope.*
> *No, I hold myself in quiet and silence,*
> *   like a little child in its mother's arms,*
> *   like a little child, so I keep myself.*
> *Let Israel hope in Yahweh*
> *   henceforth and for ever.*   Ps 131

We want to know about discernment, and the Lord wants to teach us. And so, continue to relax in prayer. Don't worry about what God might say or do. After all, we've been chosen and called His very own, so that the work God has begun in us can be brought to completion (cf., Phil 1:6). We want to learn about discernment, so let's expect that God will teach us.

As we seek the Father's will, therefore, allow the Spirit to emerge from within. God's power is there—the power of Jesus, the power of the Father's love—so expect to see it, and know it. God desires to surprise us with the Love that is within, so pray that you will be ready for the unexpected. Just as we need to be ready for the unexpected, just as we need to be ready to respond to a variety of gestures from our loved ones, so we need to be open to a variety of gestures from the Father. If the two on the road to Emmaus had readied themselves for the unexpected, they would have known the Father's will. They were not ready; they were bound to the routine. Jesus, however, desired to appear in an unexpected, yet ordinary way—through a simple conversation and the sharing of bread. They did not learn the Father's will because they did not recognize God's will present to them in Jesus.

Finally, as we relax and expect the surprise of the Father's love, we will learn God's ways. Just as a child relaxes in his/her father's arms and expects to float, so too can we learn how to swim in God's Love by following the child's example of trusting and relaxing. The Lord wants to teach us the Father's will. Of this, be certain.

This book, however, can only point the way. It is the Father who teaches us; the Father, through Jesus, Who takes us; the Father, in Jesus' Spirit, Who guides us. God will do as promised. The Father will meet us in His Son, Jesus (God's will for us) and take us beyond to the Kingdom. For this reason the Word became flesh, so that the Father's will—Jesus, the Word of Love spoken from the Father's heart—could be made known (cf., 1 Jn 1:1-4).

The Goal

The goal of discernment is to find God, and in finding God, to know God's will. Note the sequence: we first seek God, *then* God's will. Many reverse this sequence. They spend time and energy seeking to know what God wants them to do, rather than seeking God alone. Remember, we do not have to accomplish something for God to reveal His will to us. All we need do is seek God to find God's will.

The enterprise before us, therefore, has little to do with accomplishments and everything to do with discovery. For in discernment, we are meant to discover, uncover, the wholeness and the holiness of God; to grasp the very essence of the Father revealed to us in Jesus, God's Word. Such a "discovery" eventually uncovers God's will for us because in grasping Jesus, we are grasped by God. Just as a child leaps into a father's arms and clings to the father who grasps him/her tightly, so we are called to leap towards our Heavenly Father so God might grasp us tightly.

Knowing the unknowable, or the hidden answer, therefore, has little to do with discernment. Rather than being a magic system which unveils God's plan, it is the concrete process of entering the Father's life by living the life of the Risen Lord. More than asking God to enter us, we—through a life of discernment—enter God's life through Jesus, the One who is truly and totally alive in the Father.

Our entrance into Jesus' life takes place on a daily basis as we learn to recognize and identify our personal, spiritual movements: those inner promptings, attractions, etc.—often called emotions or affections—which are part of our ordinary, human experience. Unfortunately, we often seek the bolt of lightning, the mystical high, the pounding of the heart when trying to recognize the Father's will. True discernment, however, does not wait for the extraordinary, but roots itself in our ordinary, human experience. We can make this assumption because the extraordinary, i.e., Jesus, in taking on our flesh, has become ordinary (human).

Discernment, therefore, is surprisingly practical. It is the recognition of God's voice and call spoken here and now in the ordinary, everyday experience of our humanity, rather than in the esoteric, god-talk whispered in our ear during some transcendental moment.

This "human" approach to discernment should not surprise us. After all, we were made to converse with the Father who speaks His complete Word to us in the Incarnate Lord. God's language, therefore, His method of dialogue, will not be in some indecipherable code which few can comprehend. In fact, God has already chosen His language by speaking to us in the one, common denominator of our humanity, as it is lived by Christ.

In our humanity, therefore, God's will can be found, because Jesus, God's will for us, has entered into that humanity. This reality is meant to free us. Now, we can look within and find God whose Word dwells in our humanness.

Yet, God's Word does not dwell in a vacuum. Mingled with the Word, are those words and phrases which do not find their base in the Father. True discernment, therefore, teaches us to measure our inner words against the proper goal of our life, namely, choosing the Father through Jesus. More than asking whether God is leading us through our affections and inner feelings, we can now ask

whether these inner feelings and emotions are leading us
to God!

Discernment, then, is that ongoing process of conversion and transformation which separates the Eternal
Word within, from the emotions and affections which
prevent us from hearing that Word. This process, nurtured by faith, helps us to live in the Kingdom by choosing Jesus.

By learning to live a life of discernment, we will find
our human experiences pregnant with Jesus' life, pregnant with the Spirit's power, pregnant with the Father's
love through the power of Christ's cross. By learning and
living this process, we will then know how to choose God
in each situation; we will then find God's will.

How to Read This Book

The following pages give the tools needed for this
endeavor. Remember, however, that we must present to
God the openness of heart and mind that allows those
tools to accomplish their purpose. Finally, give yourself
time. When reading this book, give yourself time to famil-
iarize yourself with each of the tools described. Be patient
as you practice silence, listening, and reflective prayer.
Avoid the temptation of reading the entire book in one sitting. Far better to linger prayerfully over the chapters.
Keep in mind that discernment is a lifestyle we embrace,
not a set of formulas we memorize.

The key to discernment is silence. To relax in the Father
and to know God's will require silence. What this book
says is not important; what God says to you in silence,
however, is important. It is in the stillness, the quiet voice,

the whispers that we will sense God's tugging, pulling, and leading. While reading this book, therefore, choose silence, for just as the Eternal Word emerged from the silence of Mary's womb, so will Jesus emerge again in the silence of our hearts.

Be as generous with prayer as with silence. Suggested prayer exercises will be given in several chapters. Try to use the points given for meditation. Finally, may I suggest that you begin your search for the Father's will by praying the following prayer, or one of your own choosing which expresses your openness to the Lord's leading you as you seek God in every situation:

Father, I have decided to follow your Son;
I have decided to put aside everything and everyone
so that I might know the consuming Love
you desire to give me.
Father, I have decided to choose your Son
in every situation as best as I am able.
I only ask that you grant me
the grace and strength needed to make that choice a reality.
Let no barrier stand in my way;
let no one and no thing come between us.
Help me to keep my eyes, my heart, my very being centered
    on you,
so I might enter into your life—
a life shared with me in Jesus your Son.
Father, grant me this grace so I may abide in your heart for-
    ever.

Chapter 1

Tool #1: The Biblical View

The first tool we inspect is an historical one—looking at the biblical person's presupposition in relating to God. We do this to discover what a biblical person expected; where did he/she find God, how did he/she interpret God's responses? Simply stated, scholars tell us that biblical men and women (the people of Israel), bound to their God in a covenant experience, held a basic, faith-view of all reality. This stance leads to four assumptions.

Assumption One: God is at work in all believers drawing them to Himself.

The people of Israel believed that they encountered God on two levels: in life and in history. They were conscious that God spoke to individuals, giving them direction and guidance (cf., Gen 15), and believed that God spoke to them throughout Israel's history (e.g., Is 45). This latter expectation allowed believers to hear God's speaking and see God's self-revelation in the events of the past.

This insight formed the people of Israel into a unified body, enabling the individual to be one with all Israel, even when separated by great distances or periods of time. Hearing and responding now became a communal as well as an individual event. This insight enabled the biblical person to be there at Mt. Sinai with all God's people; to gather for prayer at the temple in Jerusalem with all God's people; to bow in worship with all God's people—past and present—saying with one voice, "Amen," in answer to the Lord's call.

The realization of this communal and individual relationship with God, opened the biblical person to hear God's Word in every event and situation encountered, either as an individual or as a member of the Israelite community. For example, whether there was defeat or victory in battle, or even a natural disaster such as famine or drought, God was speaking (cf., Deut 32).

Such an attitude enabled the biblical person to see God in the existential situation, in the now, as the experience was happening. Whether good or bad, comfortable or uncomfortable, God's Word was being spoken, His Word was near for the listening (cf., Deut 30:11-14).

The discernment process challenges us to embrace the aforementioned assumption as our own, seeing God's movement in every situation, bringing all to completion according to His plan. More than simply convincing ourselves that "everything is okay," this first assumption challenges us to remember that what we experience now is God's love for us. St. Paul assures us that everything works for the good (Rom 8:28). For us who acknowledge God's love, this really implies that we are experiencing God's love now in the events which surround us.

Such an assumption forces us to discard our own plans, dismantling the misguided hope that in the end God will finally realize our plan was the best. A life of discernment necessarily reshapes the subtle, but ill-conceived, self-assurance implicit in this attitude. After all, it is quite easy to accept and believe God is speaking to us and loving us if we have just received a raise or won the lottery. The loss of a job, the death of a spouse, the pain of an alcoholic child, however, makes it harder to accept the idea that God is somehow loving us and speaking to us in this situation. Yet, for those who believe, the now is God's loving Word for us.

Assumption Two: God speaks to us through our intellect (the Old Testament word is heart) and affections (emotions).

For this Law which I am laying down for you today is neither obscure for you nor beyond your reach. It is not in heaven, so that you need to wonder, "Who will go up to heaven for us and bring it down to us, so that we can hear and practice it?" Nor is it beyond the seas, so that you need to wonder, "Who will cross the seas for us and bring it back to us, so that we can hear and practice it?" No, the word is very near to you, it is in your mouth and in your heart for you to put into practice.

Deut 30:11-14

This passage points to a basic reality: God's Word, ever-present for our reflection, dwells within us. Regardless of our background, our state of life, our personality, the Word dwells within each of us. God dwells within, offering guidance, correction, encouragement, consolation. Using all the events of life, therefore, the Lord touches our heart and mind. His Word is constant.

For this reason, we must tune our mind and heart to God's voice as He speaks within. In Numbers 11:24-29 we see this directive in operation. Joshua did not hear God's Word being spoken because his heart and mind were not tuned into listening to someone outside his camp. Therefore, he missed hearing God's Word. In like manner, we often miss God's Word because we tune out His voice, should it come from an unexpected source, e.g., TV, non-believers, world events, etc. In each of these situations, however, God's Word is saying something to us. Yet we often ignore it because the source seems too "worldly."

When we discount these "worldly" sources, we eliminate a body of data in which our mind and heart are submerged. God is not hiding in the world or from the world making it impossible to hear Him. He has entered the world so that His voice can be heard.

Assumption Three: Evil is a reality that can work in all.

In today's society, the presence of evil has been sensationalized through movies, books, and news reports. We accept the word, "evil," although we mock the reality. Too often, the stereotype image of the devil with horns and tail has made the reality quite unbelievable. Nevertheless, evil does exist.[1]

Such a statement, however, should not lead us to the other extreme. Although evil is a reality, do not assume that an evil spirit is behind every tree and the cause of every crisis. More often than not, our own sinfulness is the "evil" present, rather than some personalized demon. The following story helps clarify this point.

Once upon a time, during the era of princes and knights, castles and serfs, there was a weary traveler seeking shelter for the night. Dusk was approaching and he was rushing to a nearby town before night ended his journey. He did not really want to stay in that town since it had a terrible reputation, but he knew that he needed some type of shelter from the wild animals that prowled the area at night. As night finally came, the traveler reached the gates. Sitting outside, however, was the devil. He knew it was the devil because he had horns and a tail.

Filled with curiosity he asked the devil, "Sir, why are you sitting here, outside the walls? This town has the reputation of being possessed by you. It is known for its evil and violent ways, and you sit here. Why are you not inside the town stirring up the evil for which you are blamed?" Twitching his tail, the devil looked at the traveler, and gave a big yawn. Garbled within the yawn was his answer to the traveler: "They don't need me in there. They're doing very well by themselves!"[2]

By taking to heart those first assumptions, the practical application of discernment will be easier for us. The process itself allows us to be conscious of God's Holy Spirit bearing witness within us through our mind and heart; it helps us to recognize God's Word spoken here and now in the events of here and now; it teaches us how to sense the Lord's presence by recognizing the confirming spirits of peace and joy as each existential event touches us. In short, the biblical person reminds us that God's voice can be recognized.

Assumption Four: Discernment is communal.

The biblical person was aware that hearing the infinitely rich word of God required the entire community. This community included those past and those present. Perhaps "tradition" best summarizes the biblical attitude. The Word of God past (tradition) confirms the Word of God present (the existential event). This takes place because God's Word within life and history has been speaking the same message throughout time; that Word dwelling within the community has been saying, "You are Mine, You are loved, You are forgiven!"

For the biblical person and for us, community has an essential place because it reminds us of the basic Word spoken. This is why sharing our heart and mind is important. In doing so, we look to see whether the Word spoken within us is the same as or resonates with the Word spoken within the entire community throughout all time.

The sharing of which I speak is not the "witnessing" or "major-truth," group dynamic sharing which is often a personal catharsis for the one sharing. The proper "sharing" in the discernment process is our reflection (intellect) on the movement of God's Spirit within (affections) and the comparison of that to God's movement within the community (tradition throughout history). We accomplish this by seeking counsel from a wise person who carries within himself/herself the roots and the traditions of the community, or by engaging in the process of discernment within a group setting.[3]

Living a life of discernment requires effort. It is a labor, a work in which we need to move wholeheartedly. It requires our learning how to listen to others differently, aware that their words are not merely an opinion but a gift from God to us now. This work always challenges us to shift gears as new insights, experiences, and chances for conversion enter our mind and heart through the minds and hearts of others.

Finally, the process of discernment requires that we be freed from our own subjectivity. Here we have the hardest work of all: to be disarmed and defenseless in the Spirit's presence.

Prayer Exercise: Discernment Examen[4]

This is a simple prayer exercise which can teach us the art of "fine-tuning" our hearts and minds to the promptings of the Spirit. It is not an examination of conscience which usually helps us to see the rightness or wrongness of our actions. Rather, it is a prayerful inspection of the inner movements and promptings (often called "spirits" by St. Ignatius) which we have felt during the day.

This type of examen, therefore, will help us recognize what was happening "inside" during those times when we put on the mind of Christ; it will help us recognize Christ in all things by pointing out how we "felt" when we chose or did not choose the Lord. The discernment examen should take approximately ten minutes when used every night.

1. Relax in the presence of God. Use a psalm or a hymn to help you.
2. Thank God for everything that the Lord has brought into your life since the day before.
3. Beg to be given the mind and heart of Jesus, to see reality as Jesus sees it.
4. Reflect prayerfully over your day by checking the "we" (what you and Jesus experienced together)

against the "I" (you alone), thus bringing to life St. Paul's insight "it is no longer I, but Christ living in me" (Gal 2:19). This emphasizes the reality of our life as a "we" (you and Jesus) not an "I."

As you reflect over the day, visualize those events about which you can say "we" (even if you were not conscious of God's presence at the time). For example, "We ate breakfast, we drove to work, we cleaned the house, we spent time with people, etc."

Recall, then, those events about which you cannot say "we." For example, "I blew up at the children, I got angry at the slow traffic, I cheated in the store, etc." As you prayerfully review the day's events in this manner, the Spirit will make you aware of the myriad ways in which God was present to you throughout the day. The Spirit will enable you to "discern" or distinguish God's touch from all the other movements, promptings and urges in your life. This, in turn, will help you become more aware of God's presence in the days ahead. This awareness will evolve into that ideal of working, playing, resting, living in Christ that St. Paul describes.

5. Renew, in love, your sorrow for ever having disappointed or offended the Father. Offer a short prayer of repentance and sorrow at this time.

6. Plan a time of prayer for tomorrow. Make it definite in length and place. Also, promise to repair any damage you may have done to others should the Lord give you the opportunity tomorrow.

7. End by praying the Our Father.

A second prayer assignment is to pray over the Old Testament passage from Deuteronomy 30:11-14. Use the following points for meditation:

1. Begin with a spontaneous prayer asking for the Lord's presence.

2. Reflect on how this passage reveals the mystery of God's plan. Think of how God's Word is given to us through the Old Testament, the New Testament, and in Jesus.

3. Pray for the specific grace to accept the Word. Pray that the Word, as it is embodied and enfleshed in Jesus, will spring to life within you.

4. Think of how the Word is near . . . not beyond you . . . not impossible to live. Let silence predominate. Don't worry about distractions; ignore them.

   Think of the different ways the Word has been spoken to you; name the people who bore the Word to you. Ask God to bless them.

   Think of the Spirit and how He brought the Word to life for you.

5. Pray to Mary. Ask her intercession, that she who brought forth the embodiment of the Word, she who carried within her person the Word himself, Jesus, will ask her Son to become part of you.

   Pray to Jesus, that he will grant you the grace to become for others a manifestation of the Word.

   Pray to the Father, that He will make you bearer, hearer and responder to the Word.

6. Slowly pray the Our Father.

7. As a final point of meditation, listen to a song that reinforces the nearness of God.[5]

---

[1] See M. Scott Peck, M.D., *People of the Lie: The Hope for Healing Human Evil* (New York: Simon and Schuster, 1983) for an eye-opening account of this truth.

[2] I heard this story many years ago but do not remember the source.

[3] See Chapter 6.

[4] Taken from notes by Fr. Armand Nigro, S.J., received during a directed retreat.

[5] One possible selection is the song, "You Are Near," from *Neither Silver Nor Gold*, by the St. Louis Jesuits. Published and distributed by Oregon Catholic Press. Phone: 1-800-LITURGY.

Chapter 2

Tool #2: An Explicit Attitude and Atmosphere of Faith

Heavenly Father; we ask for your blessing.
We know that through the power of your Son, Jesus,
you have placed within our hearts your Word of Love,
Your presence in our midst.
Help us to hear that Word;
help us to cling to it with every fiber of our being.
Help us to know that through the Word
You dwell in us, and invite us to dwell in You.

We are meant to touch and be touched by the reality of the living God: the very same man, Jesus, who 2000 years ago took upon himself our flesh and our sins. He is alive—not a concept or a myth. We are called to experience him (cf., 1 Jn 1:1-3).

In a life of discernment, our experience[1] of God is a foundation stone. Not to know God in the depth of our being, not to know the Lord's love, not to know with heartfelt conviction that Jesus is alive—here and now—for me and in me, not to know in some "sensible" way this reality is to begin a life of discernment with severe limitations.

This observation is made lest we seek someone false whose existence for us is hearsay; lest we follow someone we do not know and recognize. Experience of the crucified Lord, raised from the dead, is a necessary first step. Though manifested differently in each person's life and at various times in a person's life, faith-conviction is essential.

Where does one receive such a conviction? The answer is deceptively simple: from Jesus. The free movement of God towards humankind is definitively begun in Jesus Christ. As St. Athanasius says, "God became man so that man could become God." Supported by a community and nourished with the stillness and quiet of prayer, we proceed with conviction to the God Who already has proceeded towards us in Jesus, and continues proceeding towards us in the Spirit.

An individual's faith-conviction, therefore, goes beyond the spiritual zap of a Cursillo, a charismatic prayer meeting, or a "born-again" experience. It rests securely in the pulling, tugging and urging of the Father within our hearts. It is a gift, freely given,[2] nurtured in prayer; a gift which may come with sudden power or subtle gentleness. It is the "I am certain" experience that does not waver from experience to experience, but grounds itself on the truth of God's presence.

Perhaps, as a child you've had an experience where you strongly felt God's presence and love for you. Most of us have had such experiences, though they may have slipped our memory. For such experiences to be a faith-conviction, we need to nurture them with prayer, whether it be vocal, meditative, or a desperate cry for help. I call this latter prayer the prayer of the beggar—offered during those times when we are so low, nothing seems real, so desperate, we are forced to acknowledge that without God we cannot begin to see.[3]

From this faith-conviction emerges a faith-knowledge. We can have many powerful experiences (baptism of the Holy Spirit, Marriage Encounter, an unexplained survival in an accident, etc.) but until we begin to grasp a knowledge of Jesus in his humanity/divinity, we remain limited to an undisciplined feeling. Remaining on the experience level (affections) without incorporating the reflective level (intellect) is a charade. Experience without reflection is useless, neither sustaining life, nor leading us to the God we seek.

A danger of remaining at the level of faith-conviction is the danger of seeking experiences of God rather than seeking the God who gives those experiences. It would be like collecting love letters without ever wanting to meet the lover who writes them. Our thrust in discernment, therefore, is to move with faith-conviction to faith-knowledge, to come to know with our mind, the Lord we experience in our heart.

This faith-knowledge is rooted in Jesus, the Revelation of the Father. As it says in Mark's Gospel, "This is my Son, the Beloved. Listen to him" (Mk 9:7). Listening to Jesus, we learn about the Father; listening to Jesus, we learn the meaning of our heart's experience, which is our faith-conviction.

A life of discernment, therefore, requires study. We are not meant to operate from a solely inspirational feeling of God's presence, nor are we meant to rely on our own feelings, thoughts and ideas. If we disregard faith-knowledge as we enter the process of discernment, if we cease learning what the Father has revealed to us in Jesus, what God shows us in our heart's experience, we are inviting chaos, confusion, and our own notion of revelation to predominate.

Though Jesus is the definitive and complete Revelation of the Father, God also reveals Himself intimately and personally through our affections. Faith-knowledge helps us in this area by showing us how to sift through our emotions and follow those which lead us to the Father. These emotions (affections) vary in kind and intensity: anger, lust, joy, pride, peace, etc. They need to be clarified, separated, and integrated in such a way that they reveal to us a leaning or non-leaning toward the Father.

In today's Catholic community, our attempts to teach faith-knowledge apart from faith-conviction have created a difficulty with far-reaching consequences, e.g., the creation of a Catholic subset where people receive sacraments for cultural reasons devoid of faith reasons. On the other hand, a problem confronting some Pentecostal groups is the tendency to cling to their faith-conviction, but to disregard, as superfluous or unimportant, the whole area of faith-knowledge. A life of discernment requires both.

As we integrate faith-conviction and faith-knowledge, a third level surfaces: self-knowledge or self-awareness. This enables us to answer the question, "Who am I?" since our self-identity can be found in God's revelation of His own self to us in Jesus. To know who I am is to know how

I am seen by the Father. To know who I am is to know my name—the name by which God speaks to me.[4] This self-knowledge does not rest on our function in society or our job description. For example, we are not merely priest, or writer, or parent in God's eyes. That is our function, not our definition. We are who the Father says we are, namely, His child.

Growth in self-knowledge is important, for with it we can uncover what is going on within our being. For example, as we learn about our sinfulness, we will learn that the Lord frees us from sin; as we learn of our shortcomings, we will learn that the Lord fills the gaps; as we learn "where we're at" in a given relationship or situation, we will learn that God wishes to draw us to "where He's at."

St. Paul states it this way:

> *In the abundance of his glory may he, through his Spirit, enable you to grow firm in power with regard to your inner self, so that Christ may live in your hearts through faith, and then, planted in love and built on love, with all God's holy people you will have the strength to grasp the breadth and the length, the height and the depth; so that, knowing the love of Christ, which is beyond knowledge, you may be filled with the utter fullness of God.*   Eph 3:16-19

In this passage Paul seems to imply that our hidden self, our inner being, must emerge (self-knowledge) so that we might know the love of Christ, which is beyond faith-knowledge and faith-conviction. This is a growth process which reveals the fullness of Christ as our faith-conviction and faith-knowledge allow the self to emerge.

For this reason we need never be afraid of knowing ourselves, or of asking who we are in the light of our experience and knowledge of the Risen Lord. It is for this reason that acts of penance have always been part of the Church's tradition. In the act of penance, we are able to discover the Lord's plan of redemptive love working through our sinfulness. Penance allows the Spirit of God to strip us bare, so the "real self" can emerge.

To confront our inner self without the Lord, without faith-conviction and faith-knowledge, would be a frightening experience. We would find little power within ourselves to change. St. Paul expressed this frustration in his letter to the Romans:

> *I do not understand my own behavior; I do not act as I mean to, but I do things that I hate. While I am acting as I do not want to, I still acknowledge the Law as good, so it is not myself acting, but the sin which lives in me. And really, I know of nothing good living in me—in my natural self, that is—for though the will to do what is good is in me, the power to do it is not: the good thing I want to do, I never do; the evil thing which I do not want—that is what I do. But every time I do what I do not want to, then it is not myself acting, but the sin that lives in me.*
>
> *So I find this rule: that for me, where I want to do nothing but good, evil is close at my side. In my inmost self I dearly love God's law, but I see that acting on my body there is a different law which battles against the law in my mind. So I am brought to be a prisoner of that law of sin which lives inside my body.*

What a wretched man I am! Who will rescue me from this body doomed to death? God—thanks be to him— through Jesus Christ our Lord.   Rom 7:15-25

By growing in self-knowledge we begin to realize that the process of discernment, the process of seeking God, requires our putting aside everything and everyone.

For how long?	A lifetime.
How much effort?	Every effort.
How can we begin since we have so many other things to do?	We do not have anything else to do except to be stripped, be naked, be disarmed, be vulnerable so the God who loves us can clothe us with His glory.

Two helpful books which expand upon this idea of self-knowledge are Walter Ciszek's, *He Leadeth Me*[5] and Corrie TenBoom's *The Hiding Place*.[6] These books relate the powerful life stories of a man and a woman, who discovered that a person cannot be clothed with Christ unless he or she is first stripped naked. This stripping, however, cannot take place if we do not grow in self-knowledge.

As we move from (1) the experience of God (faith-conviction) to (2) a faith-knowledge of Jesus, towards (3) a knowledge of ourselves (self-knowledge) we begin to grow in wisdom, which helps us in life's practical situations integrate these three elements. St. James exhorts us to pray specifically for that gift[7] which gives us the ability to "put it all together." St. Luke, however, reminds us that the gift, though freely given still exacts a price.[8]

The reason wisdom "costs," is simple. Entering into the life process of discernment, trying day by day to recognize God in our midst, attempting to seek God in every situation, often calls us to follow paths that are unexpected and sometimes undesirable. What foolishness to know where God is and not to go! What foolishness to put off until tomorrow that which we discern the Lord wants today!

When the Lord gives us the grace of wisdom, therefore, we need to accept it. This is why self-knowledge is crucial. To know our weaknesses and strengths, the ways the Lord moves within us as compared to the ways our human spirit or an evil spirit moves within, will help us respond to the wisdom given. In the life of discernment, wisdom points out the direction, but we ourselves must choose to go there. Wisdom will lead us towards the Paschal Mystery, but through our self-knowledge we need first to acknowledge what must be purified.

Another image used in Luke is that of a king going off to battle.[9] He must first know his strengths (self-knowledge) before he can execute the plan (wisdom) which will guide him in the battle. We, too, must pay the price for wisdom—the willingness to sacrifice the illusion of self as we seek our real self in God.

Part of the inner struggle with living the life of discernment is not our uncertainty regarding a direction, but rather our uncertainty that the direction chosen will really lead us to the God we seek. Hannah Hurnard's classic, *Hind's Feet on High Places*[10] shows, through a simple allegory, what might occur if we are willing to pay the price—despite the doubts and fears which tell us "No," despite the fact that the Lord's "wisdom" does not always seem that wise.[11]

At this point, everything might seem too theological or speculative to be practical or real; it might seem beyond our grasp and comprehension. For this reason, I invite you to practice with a prayer exercise so that you can begin to "hear" God's voice, begin to know "who you are" before Him and recognize His calling you by name.

Name of Grace

And now, thus says Yahweh,
he who created you, Jacob,
who formed you, Israel:
Do not be afraid, for I have redeemed you;
I have called you by your name, you are mine.   Is 43:1-2

A way that God speaks to us, both individually and as a people, is by calling us by name. To live a life of discernment, therefore, requires that we know our name— our "nickname" through which God gets our attention. We might call this our Name of Grace. Knowing this name is important in discovering who we are in God's eyes, not in the eyes of the world. The world already gives us a name: carpenter, activist, sister, mother, lawyer, etc. That is not the name we want to hear; that is not the name which gives us our definition. We need to hear our real name, our true definition according to the plan of God.

This emphasis on name is rooted in Scripture and in our own experience. In the Old Testament, for example, the people were not allowed to use Yahweh's name because Yahweh did not receive His definition or meaning from the people. He was simply He Who is—beyond control of His creation. In the New Testament, Jesus changes Simon's name to Peter—the Rock upon which Jesus built the Church.

We have seen in our own lives how important a name can be. Perhaps you have noticed children arguing over a certain decision. Suddenly one child tells the other, "Mommy told me I could do it this way." Suddenly, by using a name, the situation changes. The child wielding the name, "Mommy," now has power and control. So it is with us and the Lord. As we come to know God's name for us, we will have power in the situation because we will see how the Lord is calling us in that situation.

When listening for your personal Name of Grace, listen with the heart, not with the head. For example, I discovered my personal Name of Grace while strumming a guitar, trying to fashion words to a simple melody that was in my mind. I can't tell when it became clear, I only know that it did. Now when I pray, I remain attentive to the Lord calling me by my Name of Grace, "child-of-My-heart." In the most difficult situations, I am assured of God's presence when I "hear" my Name. This may or may not change the situation. That is not important. All that matters is the assurance that God is there.

To discover our Name of Grace requires patience. Sometimes it emerges in bits and pieces, and then suddenly we realize the Lord's been saying that name all along! A helpful technique is to inspect our life and see how the Lord has already been speaking to us. The following questions may be of some assistance.[12]

1. What are my favorite images of God? (Rock, Father, etc.)
2. What do I look like because of God?
3. Who is the God to whom I pray most often: Father, Son, Spirit?
4. Which of God's names means most to me?
5. Under which of God's attributes does the Lord most clearly reveal Himself to me?
6. Which are my favorite passages from Scripture?
7. Which beatitude attracts me most? Which gift of the Spirit? Which fruit of the Spirit?
8. What is my favorite liturgical feast?
9. Under what aspect has Christ chiefly presented himself to me for my loving and faithful response?
    Suffering Servant of God
    The Eldest of many brothers
    High Priest and Universal King
    Savior and Redeemer
    The Alpha and Omega
    The Way, the Truth, the Life
    The Prince of Peace
    Loving Bridegroom
    The Living Word
    The Risen Lord, etc.

Prayer Exercise: Samuel 7:18-19

1. Ask God's blessing in the preparatory prayer.
2. Think of the mystery of God's plan. Remember that God incorporates you into this plan; that He contin-

ues to converse with you as He continues to hold all things in Himself. Let that privilege lift your spirit.

3. Pray specifically that the Lord will give you the grace to hear your Name of Grace. If the questions above are helpful, use them.

4. Reflect upon the following points:
   —Remember your nothingness, except that the Lord has spoken you into existence.
   —Recall the many promises that the Lord has made and fulfilled for you already. Let God remind you of the times He was in your life.
   —Make a list of the promises yet to be fulfilled. Pray for the patience to wait with hope.
   —Make a timeline to record the different moments in your life when you saw grace develop. In doing this, pray with expectant faith that you will receive a revelation from the Lord which will enable you to sense where and how God has been working.

5. End with prayer
   —Ask Mary to intercede that Jesus will speak clearly to you.
   —Ask the help of Jesus in hearing the name his Father has given you. Ask also for the grace to be true to that name. (Remember that you are only who God says you are; to be other than this is to live a lie.)

---

[1] NB Your experience is not necessarily the same as mine, although it is the same God we experience. All valid Christian experiences should somehow resound with the experience of the first witnesses, the apostles.

[2] cf. Jn 6:44; Matthew 11:25-27.

[3] *The Autobiography of St. Ignatius Loyola with Related Documents*, translated by Joseph F. O'Callaghan, edited with Introduction and Notes by John C. Olin (Hagerstown, New York: Harper & Row, 1974), Section 23.

[4] The upcoming section, "Name of Grace" explains this more fully.

[5] Walter Ciszek, *He Leadeth Me* (Garden City, New York: Doubleday Image, 1975).

[6] Corrie TenBoom, *The Hiding Place* (Grand Rapids, MI: Revell, 1974).

[7] James 1:5-6.

[8] Luke 14:25-27.

[9] Luke 14:31-33.

[10] Hannah Hurnard, *Hind's Feet on High Places* (Wheaton, IL: Tyndale House Publishers, Inc., 1976).

[11] Cf., I Corinthians 1:18-30.

[12] Taken from material distributed at the Jesuit Center for Spiritual Growth in Wernersville, PA.

Chapter 3

Tool #3: Personal Anamnesis

And as they were eating he took bread, and when he had said the blessing he broke it and gave it to them. "Take it," he said, "this is my body." Then he took a cup, and when he had given thanks he handed it to them, and all drank from it, and he said to them, "This is my blood, the blood of the covenant, poured out for many." Mk 14:22-24

Chapter 1 established the basic assumptions which would be useful in living a life of discernment. In describing these "tools," we presented discernment as a process which goes beyond our knowing what to do or what to accomplish in a particular situation. We saw that discernment was a life in God—not a God somewhere "out there," but One present in our human experience because of Jesus. All this is a growth process during which we learn to choose on the level of faith those inner affections which lead us towards the Kingdom—the place of transformation in Christ.

In addition, we learned that God has singled out our uniqueness by endowing each of us with a Name of Grace, that special nickname by which we recognize God's voice. Discovering our Name of Grace requires prayer, silence, discipline, and a desire to see and hear the

Lord in our human experiences. These are the initial building blocks needed for entering a life of discernment.

We now look at the third tool needed for a life of discernment. The technical term is personal anamnesis, an impressive phrase which simply means remembering. In living a life of discernment, in seeking God and His will, we must learn how to return to our first moments of grace. One might say that we have to remember our roots, our story.

The Church returns daily to its first moment of grace through the Eucharist. Is it not true that through the Eucharist we are at the foot of Calvary; we are at the death of Jesus on the cross? In some way we are there— present—just as John, Mary and the other women were present.

Personal anamnesis, therefore, is our going back in time and reliving that experience of grace in our own being. Think of a tree: it grows above its roots but never outgrows them. We, too are called to grow above our past experiences, whether they be Marriage Encounter, a "born-again" experience, Cursillo, etc., although we are not going to outgrow them. This "recalling" allows our past experiences to nourish us in the present just as the roots nourish the tree that grows above it.

One living a life of discernment treasures these graces—not for the sake of seeking or clinging to an experience— but rather for the purpose of becoming refreshed and nourished anew. St. Peter says, "Try even harder to make God's call and choice of you a permanent experience."[1] Our ability to remember is personal anamnesis.

In prayerful reflection we drink anew at the springs of past graces. Entering into the quiet and solitude of prayer, we encounter this gift of remembering, this grace, which bears the mark of eternity. Just as our hearts are filled with joy when we recall a treasured memory, so remembering our past graces refreshes us again and again. Perhaps the reason is that Jesus, Emmanuel, God-with-us, Gift of the Father endures forever in His Spirit. For God does not give us His gifts in vain. They do not disappear or evaporate like a mist but are part of God's self-giving, since all graces spring from Him.

The Gift or Grace from God is Jesus in His Holy Spirit—an eternal presence. Personal anamnesis can help us integrate that eternal moment of God's speaking His Word to us, here and now; it can help us realize that every moment with Jesus is a never ending beginning—new, fresh, vibrant.

This process refreshes us by allowing our latent knowledge and experiences of God to resurface. For example, why do we reread love letters if not to remember the experience of receiving them and savor them once again in the present? Through personal anamnesis we discover that grace endures. It is eternal because Jesus, the source of grace, is eternal. This is why Jesus is called Emmanuel, God-with-us. He, who is the unique Gift and Grace of the Father, is ever present with us in His Spirit.

Personal anamnesis is illustrated throughout the Old Testament whenever God's people were called to remember what the Lord had done for them, e.g., the Ten Commandments, the Exodus, the Sinai Covenant. This remembering was, in fact, a crucial element in the renewal of the Israelite people. Through it, there was a real participation in the past event by remembering it in the present. The Passover ritual is another example of this mindset in action.

This should not surprise us. The very idea of past, present and future which we call time, is something humankind has invented. For God, there is no time, there is only present. What seems past to us is ever-present to God.

As we enter the process of personal anamnesis, we literally shatter time by stepping outside our own concepts and entering into God-time: the eternal now, where past, present and future are one point in God. We experience this reality within our own Catholic tradition whenever we celebrate Eucharist. For in the Eucharist, we celebrate more than a reenactment of an historic event, we step into eternity by sharing a moment of the past here in the present.

The same is true for sacraments wherein Jesus is present now, in the way he was present then, because they are one and the same way, and it is one and the same God who is present. This is true for our liturgical experiences as well.

Grace, therefore, is forever. It is a moment in history that becomes history. It is a moment in time that becomes timeless. This is how Jesus is for us. He is the Word made flesh, the Word of Love spoken in time from the Father's heart. By speaking that Word in time, that Word revealed itself as timeless, ever present to us all.

Entering deeply into a life of discernment requires that we learn how to enter into the timelessness of Jesus, ever present, and the timelessness of God's love, forgiveness, grace, power and Spirit. Through this process true renewal takes place because we draw upon the enduring grace of the Father already given in the Word Incarnate; we draw from the infinite reservoir of God-with-us.

Those times when we pray for "more grace," therefore, are actually contradictions since the Father has already filled us to overflowing. Our prayer, in reality, is a prayer to respond to the grace already present. Through personal anamnesis we are aware of this truth, and so reflect upon the past in order to enter the eternity of the present moment.

Prayer Exercise: Becoming comfortable with the tool of personal anamnesis requires time and patience. The following exercise will get you started.

Try to locate, by memory, those deep reservoirs of grace which spring from our souls, one for each of our deepest religious experiences. Locate any one of these experiences and allow it to flow into the present with its entire composite of feelings, moods, thoughts, convictions, commitments and joys. Such an exercise is meant to refresh us, not entrap us in the past. Remember, we are going beyond the concept of time into the timelessness of grace.

Try using this exercise after receiving Communion. Spend about twenty minutes engaged in this process. Ask for the specific grace of remembering. The following questions are suggestions which may help you make this contact:

    1. My first awakening to the realization that God loves me.

2. My deepest experience of God's forgiveness.

3. The day I first heard God's call "Follow Me."

4. My most cherished experience of God in prayer.

5. My most intimate experience of God in the Eucharist.

6. The day, the hour, I discovered God as my personal Savior.

7. My most wonderful finding of God in nature.

8. My most profound discovery of God in another.

9. My most vivid religious dream.

10. Other experiences too personal to categorize.

---

[1] 2 Peter 1:10 TEV.

Chapter 4

Tool #4: Obedience

Heavenly Father, we come to you asking for the
grace of obedience.
We know that your Son Jesus beckons us to live in
you,
to be one with you,
to abide in you,
so that we might experience
the fullness of life found in your Son.
Help us to hear that call,
and respond to it.
Soften our hearts until we are pliable
in your loving hands.
Open our ears to your voice which says,
"Come, you are mine."
Father, we thank you
for giving us the means to this end
through the loving power of your Son,
present to us in his Spirit.

Through a life of discernment we realize the need for wholeness (or holiness), if we are to find the God we seek. Wholeness, however, does not come automatically. We first need to recognize our brokenness. The reason is obvious: if we do not know brokenness, we would think we were whole. If we thought we were already whole, we would not seek wholeness—we would not seek God.

Unfortunately, many people realize their brokenness, but then seek God the problem-solver, rather than God the healer of brokenness. Such a step leads to confusion because God did not come to solve our problems. He came so we could share His life. Through the Incarnation, the Lord already entered our life; now, we are called to complete the process by entering his.

To live a life of discernment, therefore, is to live our life in the Lord. He alone is the one who is truly alive, not you or I. In fact, we can be considered alive only to the degree that we are alive in him. This is what discernment shows us: seeking wholeness of life by being alive in Jesus. Perhaps we might look at it this way: in all of creation, there is only one person who is really alive—Jesus the Lord. He alone is raised from the dead, living vibrantly and intimately in the Father. Not to be alive in him, therefore, is to be dead! This is why St. Paul writes,

> *You have stripped off your old behavior with your old self, and you have put on a new self which will progress towards true knowledge the more it is renewed in the image of its Creator; . . . There is only Christ: he is everything and he is in everything.* Col 3:9-11[1]

Who is this new one if it is not Jesus? We are called to put on Christ, to become him, to enter him.

Discernment, therefore, allows our heart's need—our need for oneness with Jesus—to be realized through our rootedness in God. We find God, therefore, to the degree that this process takes place. Then, in finding God, we will know God's will.

What is God's will? To be His—totally His. God wills that we be completely consumed by the fire of His love. God wants us to return to the natural beauty of His creation.

How? One word sums it up: obedience. We may be frightened by that word, because we misunderstand its meaning. Some people actually avoid using the word when referring to marriage, or authority, or the Gospel's teaching. They think its use implies blindness, foolishness, lack of self-worth on the part of the one obeying.

In fact, however, the word is quite beautiful and meaningful. It tells us "to listen to." The type of listening implied, however, is unlike the listening you expect from a private in the army. It is far more subtle and gentle. In its root, the word means to give ear to, to strain in hearing what is being whispered on the other side of a wall. Obedience means to give ear to someone's heartbeat; to place our ear on his/her chest and quietly count the heartbeats.

Obedience for us, then, is our listening to the Father's heartbeat, listening to God's desire for us; listening in silence with head, heart, and faith mingled together. Herein we find the practical manifestation of love. In addition, through this obedient stance, two levels of communication emerge: the prophetic word and the existential word. Together, they can indicate for us the Word of God spoken here and now.

The Prophetic Word

In the life of discernment, the prophetic word goes beyond the charismatic gift often manifested in prayer meetings; it goes beyond a mere foretelling of the future, or speaking in the first person.[2] Provided those words are in accord with Church teaching and Scripture, they should be pondered with head and heart joined by faith. However, in a life of discernment, important prophetic words are spoken also in the lives of our saints: the Mother Teresa's, John XXIII's, Dorothy Day's, Michael Crosby's, Joan Chittister's, etc. Though these spoken prophetic words tend to leave us uncomfortable, they are powerful words from God because they strip us of our compromising views of the Gospel and reveal the naked Word of God in all its power and glory actually working in human life.

Embracing a life of discernment, therefore, challenges us to hear and acknowledge these prophetic words. Though they may make us uncomfortable and seem beyond us, though we try at times to rationalize the challenge, they need to be heard and obeyed.

The Existential Word

This word is the one encountered every day: the now word heard on TV, read in the newspapers, etc. In a sense, it is a sign of the times, there for all to see. As with the prophetic word, we are to sift, separate and differentiate when the existential word is heard. It is not an absolute truth just as the prophetic word is not an absolute truth. Looking at how this "now" word harmonizes with Scripture and the teaching of the Church, then joining it to the prophetic word spoken in the lives of the saints among us, will give a good idea of what God is saying to us now.

The following example shows this process in action. Newspapers, government agencies, people all around us, sense that things are getting worse in our economy: prices are skyrocketing, goods are becoming scarce, money is getting harder to save. This is the existential word. On the other hand, we hear the prophetic word: people striving to live in small Christian communities, e.g., the Missionary Sisters of Charity or Sojourners community, living a life of simplicity and working for the poor and social justice. Put these two words together and we "hear" God saying that believers will have to learn how to live with less and share more as we strive to work with God's Spirit in bringing about the Kingdom.

There are three areas where we might hear the prophetic and existential word.

Prayer

This refers to the contemplative type of listening, the pondering, wherein the Word can be heard. Mary, who pondered the message of the angel, exemplifies this prayer. Helpful in this area is the daily discernment examen, explained in Chapter 1. The proper, inner attitude, therefore, goes beyond "praying." It is an attitude of the heart.

Spiritual direction also helps in realizing this prayer: the guidance of a wise person who can say to us, "It's good, but not God"; someone who can help us understand what we are hearing.

In this prayer context, four things emerge over a period of time: we become aware of what is going on within our spirit; we learn how to express (announce) what is happening within our heart (faith-sharing); we grow in our ability to accept it as part of a process working within; and, we become motivated to choose to act one way or another, according to our inner movements.

Hearing the prophetic and existential word, therefore, will bear fruit as we ponder and integrate these four a's into our lives. I think of Sister Jane Reilly from the Diocese of Rockville Centre. For many years she has been working in the diocesan mission in the Dominican Republic. Her involvement there did not happen overnight. She first had to be *aware* of what was happening within her spirit—the promptings of the Spirit which led her to her vocation. In addition, she needed to be aware of the needy people around her—those crying out for Jesus. Her awareness, however, had to be *announced* so others could also sense what was occurring. Having realized it was from the Lord, she had to *accept* the process taking place within. Once this acceptance occurred, *action* followed—she chose to devote her life to the poor in the Dominican Republic.

Talents/needs

God's grace is specifically tailored for each person. From the universal gift of Jesus and the Spirit comes the unique, specialized grace offered to each individual. It is quite true that grace builds on nature, which is why God's grace so perfectly suits each of us. God has placed within our nature various talents and needs which, when touched by grace, will fulfill us and lead us to Him.

For example, we may become aware of certain personal growth needs, such as the need to be in a Christian community. When we accept this need as coming from God (i.e., it is not an evil desire, or one that would lead us from the Lord), God, Who placed it there, will use it to bring about His plan for us and others. St. Ignatius needed to live in unity with his brothers, hence the formation of the Society of Jesus. Charles de Foucauld needed to live in poverty, hence the start of the Little Brothers of Jesus.

Perhaps a widow or widower realizes she/he needs companionship. Nothing is wrong with this need. It does not imply a weakness or a deficiency. With faith in God, that person might look and see how this need could be used by God—perhaps through the formation of a St. Monica's Club, where widows and widowers gather for community and ministry. Although we may not think we have the ability, our need may reveal our ability.

Environment

The life of discernment will bear fruit only as we look at our surroundings: the people, things, cultures in which we are situated. If, for example, we have a wife and four children, it is unlikely that God's Word to us will be to enter the Trappists. It may seem like an outlandish example, but everyone has experienced those strong leadings which challenge us to move in unusual directions. Or, perhaps, we are living in a posh neighborhood. It is unlikely that the Lord would ask us to open a soup kitchen in that neighborhood since the environment does not warrant such a response. God may ask us to sell what we have, or to feed the poor, etc., but the environment needs to be considered when planning any active response to the Lord.

Christ Crucified in the Service of Others

What is the common denominator or criterion? John 15:12-13: "Love one another, as I have loved you. No one can have greater love than to lay down his life for his friends." Restated, one might say, "Christ crucified in the service of others." The Christ crucified, however, is not the Christ who has already died for us. The Christ crucified is the Christ who dwells within—the Christ in me, crucified for the service of others.

We are meant to do as Jesus did. He saved others by his death on the cross. When speaking of God's will, therefore, when speaking of seeking God alone, this becomes the common denominator: being stripped, so others can be served. Only when this process can take place, should we proceed in a particular direction. When it cannot take place, we should stop, look and listen again.

How Do We Come to This Knowledge?

A basic principle in a life of discernment is to begin with what we know, moving from clarity to clarity. By beginning with obedience, for example, we will then experience "light," clarity. As Isaiah 55:3 tells us: "Pay attention, come to me; listen, and you will live." Through obedience, light emerges.

The light, which we experience, will then lead us to truth. Jesus says it clearly in John 8:12: "I am the light of the world; anyone who follows me will not be walking in the dark but will have the light of life." Jesus does not say,

"I am a light," but "I am the light." Anyone, sinner or saint, who follows, will know the light; anyone, who is obedient, will know the truth.

John 8:31-32 points out that this Truth, who is Jesus, will lead to freedom: "If you make my word your home . . . you will come to know the truth, and the truth will set you free." This freedom is not to be identified with license. It is, rather, the freedom to be his, the freedom to worship him, the freedom to accept his embrace. It is the freedom to look at the world shrouded in darkness and say, "No," and to look toward Jesus the Light and say, "Yes."

Such freedom comes as we have grasped the Truth and been grasped by the Truth. Such freedom comes when we see the Light and follow. Such freedom comes as we choose to act: "Is a lamp brought in to be put under a tub or under the bed?" (Mk 4:21). In this—the choosing to act, the response of love towards others—we find God.

Throughout a life of discernment the Holy Spirit is working. His job? To remind us of everything; to take our mind and make it new; to re-shape and reform us. The old (mind) is gone and the new (Christ's mind) emerges. Of what does the Spirit remind us? Of the Father's love and forgiveness; that Jesus dwells within and that we are freed by his blood. The Spirit reminds us that we are God's and God's alone.

Besides moving from clarity to clarity, we come to this knowledge by uncovering God in all creation (see Rom 8). In that discovery, we realize that all we encounter is necessarily God's will. This may seem to contradict previous remarks. However, a life of discernment reveals that though our present experience is the best for us and can lead us to the Kingdom, not everything we experience is sent by God to take us to the Kingdom.

It may seem a subtle distinction, yet it remains important. Some experiences lead us to the Father because of His marvelous ways and mercy, not because they are "good" experiences as such. We are bombarded by many experiences, some good, some bad. To assume that God forces us to endure some of them, denies our freedom to choose and respond to them. Better for us to say that God uses all experiences to draw us to Himself.

A death in the family. Did God plan it so we would experience tragedy? Our spouse loses his/her job. Did God arrange it to see how we would act? More than likely, the answer is, "no"; more than likely our training says, "yes." The fact is, however, that God uses these experiences to bring about the best, and because God uses them, they are the best. A contradiction? No. Merely the mystery of God's love in our midst—light and darkness, death and life.

We must realize, then, that God will grace us here and now by giving us the ability to go to Him. We find God in our response. For example, a person who loses a job can respond with anger and depression, blaming God, or he/she can respond with searching and hope, trusting that the Lord is holding and loving him/her. The first response sees a curse, and does not see God though verbally God is "accepted"; the second response sees a gift, not yet discovered.

An important distinction, then, is how are we present to God (our response), not how is God present to us. Too often, we simply say, "Praise God," bow our heads in pious submission and deny the reality of our pain and doubt. Such an approach will not help us to find God, nor will it nurture a life of discernment. How we respond in the situation is what leads us to God. Denial of the reality merely denies the God within the reality.

God is already present to us. That is the fact. How God is present will be covered in a later chapter. For now, we will focus our attention on our presence to Him, our response to Him in everyday situations. A life of discernment helps us to perceive these ways of responding by entering the lifestyle of Jesus on the level of faith. St. Ignatius is a guide here because his personal experience was one of pondering the different "spirits,"[3] feelings, and ways he felt God was present to him. By responding in the proper direction, he found (or lost) God.

Tool #5: Interior Freedom

In order to answer the question, "How are we present to God?" we must be free. To help in checking our freedom level, several areas have been listed for reflection. Remember that no person is free in all these areas. Our entire life is the process of continued dying to self so that the freedom we seek may be realized.

1. Given our stronger inclination toward one choice rather than another, are we willing to accept the possibility that even the choice towards which we are less inclined might be the Word of God addressed to us here and now? In short, are we willing to admit that what we want may not be what God wants?

2. Have we consciously or unconsciously dismissed any of our possible choices as a means of fulfilling the goals God has set for us? This often crops up when we are discerning a vocation, choosing a major life adjustment such as moving our family, as well as choosing our involvement in a parish ministry. For example, a person might say, "Lord, I want to know how you want me to serve, but I don't want you to ask me to help out doing. . . ."

3. Do we fully intend to follow God's Word even before it is discovered, or is our decision and enthusiasm suspended until it is known? This is crucial. Too often we want to see if God's will strikes our fancy before we decide to follow it.

4. Do we really believe that God is concerned in the matter to have a Word to speak, or do we think that He is completely indifferent to any alternative that might be chosen? In other words, do we really believe that God cares?

5. Do we distrust our mere human efforts to find our goals and utilize the means to achieve them? We need to be on our guard, lest we think that God does not use human means to accomplish His end. Remember, Jesus is human. He became human so that the goal of the Father might be achieved.

6. Do we believe that others associated with us are truly willing to be led by God and are sincerely trying to be open to God's Spirit? Can we trust?

7. Does our mistrust of God, or others, or even ourselves make us fearful, timid and cautious in the search and choice of alternatives?

8. Can we commit ourselves beforehand to the discerning group's final choice (unless it is disconfirmed by just authority or by our own experience in carrying it out)?

9. Are we indifferent to all except that to which God is calling?

10. Are we ready to counter, by intense prayer, any desire we might hold which could impede or block the Word of God?

11. Can we accept the fact that God might not choose to speak through the most humanly efficient agent or process to make decisions?

12. Are we willing to name, own and examine our thoughts, emotions and feelings in order to assess the possibility of self-deception in discerning God's Word?

13. Are we aware of past failures, our lack of freedom and our ever present need for conversion and purification?

14. Are we aware of our fears and ready to renounce them?

Prayer Exercise #1: Read Romans 8:28-30.

1. Offer the usual preparatory prayer.

2. Think of the mystery of God's plan for you that what you experience is the best for you now, that you are held in the arms of a loving Father Who will never abandon you.

3. Pray for the specific grace to see the best in life, no matter what circumstances may be confronting

you. If there is a particular situation on your mind, focus on it.

4. Points for meditation:

—Imagine how disoriented and frightening your life would be if the Lord had not called you his own.

—Reflect on the ways you are the image of Jesus— not the ways you are supposed to be an image of him.

—Thank the Lord for healing you through his Cross and Resurrection. Thank him for sharing his glory with you, the glory of his death and Resurrection.

5. Final prayer.

—Pray to Mary, asking her for the grace you need to accept the Lord in your life, as she accepts the Lord in her life.

—Pray to Jesus, asking him for the grace to allow you to enter more completely into his life.

—Pray to the Father in heaven for the above graces.

6. End with the Our Father.

Prayer Exercise #2

Reflect upon the points regarding Interior Freedom. Pray specifically for the grace needed to gain a particular freedom you find lacking in your life.

---

[1] See also Eph 4:22-24.

[2] For an explanation of the charismatic gift called prophecy consult Donald Gee, *Concerning Spiritual Gifts*, (Springfield, MO: Gospel Publishing House, 1972); for an exposition of the biblical understanding of prophecy, see John L. McKenzie, S.J., *Dictionary of the Bible* (New York: Macmillan Publishing Co., Inc., 1965).

[3] When using the word "spirits' we are not speaking exclusively of evil spirits, i.e., personal beings which have been traditionally linked with Satan and his band of fallen

angels—although the word does not exclude that possibility. In the broader definition, however, we are speaking of internal spirits, i.e., our affections, human feelings, desires, etc. Jealously, for example, would be a type of "spirit" in this context, since it is an inner movement which leads us in a particular direction. Joy, anger, lust, peace, etc., are other examples of "spirits" in the life of discernment. To know and name these "spirits" are important because they move us toward or away from Jesus. For example, once the "spirit" of jealousy is named and acknowledged, we can realize the freedom of choosing our response rather than the frustration of feeling forced to respond. By choosing to reject or accept the direction in which the inner "spirit" is leading, we can grow in strength and holiness and find God.

Chapter 5

Preparation for Decision-Making

A life of discernment is the ongoing process of our life in Jesus. During this process, there will be times when we must make decisions and choices. This action of decision-making is, in fact, no more than an intensified period of prayer within a prayer process already in motion. Thinking that a person suddenly decides to discern is misleading, especially if the person is not striving to live a life of discernment.

Experience has shown that the decision-making aspect of discernment, i.e., the choosing "yes" or "no" in a particular situation, becomes easier as the life of discernment permeates our everyday routine. This is quite reasonable since the actual decision-making time is nothing more than our focusing on those inner movements or forces that are generating and have been generated throughout our life.

The example which comes to mind is that of a magnifying glass. When a person wants to burn a hole in a leaf, she/he focuses the sun through the lens until a flame appears. This technique works when the rays of light are "gathered" on the lens and properly focused on the leaf. If there is no light or if the focus is incorrect, no flame emerges. So it is with decision-making in the life of discernment: our life in Jesus (the shining son) must be focused (the gathering of rays on the lens) in order to produce a decision (the flame).

Think, also, of a cup of tea. No one prepares a cup of tea by placing the tea bag in cold water. Boiling water is needed. So it is with decision-making in our life of discernment: we must be boiling in our life in Jesus (prayer, discernment examen, interior freedom, etc.), if we intend to make a decision in accord with God's will.

Patience and perseverance are important. A person cannot decide that she/he will seek interior freedom or a life of prayer in the morning, so that x, y, and z can be decided in the afternoon. We cannot bypass the normal, Christian growth process, i.e., dying to self. In fact, the more remote a person is from this growth process of dying to self, the less she/he will be able to perceive God in the situation at hand.

The Gift of Discernment

At this point it might be helpful to distinguish between discernment as a life process and discernment as a charismatic gift. The latter refers to a special charism which graces the entire Church. This charism, or gift of the Spirit, helps a community differentiate between evil spirits and good spirits. Very often, an individual within a community framework manifests the gift so that another individual or group will know whether God is or is not moving in a particular situation.

Unfortunately, some perceive the gift of discernment to be a magic formula or pipeline to God. Such people seek out those claiming the gift, in order to "know what God wants." This attitude is dangerous because a person or group can be manipulated without being aware that the gift of discernment is not operating. Just because an individual claims the gift, does not mean that she/he has the gift. "But Father," one might say, "I prayed for the gift. I can tell I have it." Such a conviction is based on inexperience and a lack understanding. It is the Church (i.e., God's people), that has the gift of discernment. Individuals manifest it according to God's plan, to the degree in which they are living a life in Jesus, not by the persistence of inner voices, special signs, or intense feelings. The signs indicating the validity of such a gift have been stated before: allegiance to Scripture and Church teaching, willingness to die to self in the service of others and a life-style centered in the Lord.

Properly used, the gift of discernment enables the individual or group to see the Lord's actions in a particular situation, thereby allowing a choice to be made. This gift, however, is not meant to brow-beat or pressure a person into submission. It is not meant to manipulate or force an issue because "God has told me." The gift, properly used, respects the integrity of the other by avoiding debate or clever maneuvering.

In summary, we might say that the gift of discernment is used by an individual for another person or group, while a life of discernment is that growth process through which all believers can learn how to choose the Lord in their daily lives. The gift may operate as a unique grace given in a time of need for an individual's or group's growth, while a life of discernment is a process that does not rely on extraordinary moments of illumination.

Three Assumptions for Proper Discernment

1. While gathering and inspecting the data needed for the decision-making process, we need the entire community to hear the infinitely rich Word of God. This "community" reaches beyond our prayer group, parish council, family, etc. It includes the Christian community through all time.

The Father has spoken one Word to us. That Word, Jesus, is the same yesterday, today and tomorrow. Throughout all ages this Word existed, and then in time, was made flesh for us in the Incarnation. This is why we need the entire community to hear this Word of God— Infinity become flesh. We might call this "community hearing," our tradition, i.e., how our community has responded to the Word through time.

Thinking that individually we can hear that Word in the vacuum of our lives is self-deceptive. Only by listening with all God's people—the saints through all time— can we be sure that our hearing is "fine tuned." God does not speak in an individualized vacuum. God speaks to a people, calls a people, forms a people. To seek God, therefore, and to know His will is to know how God has spoken to His people, and then to compare our own inner words or interior sense to those already spoken and experienced in history.

This does not negate or deny the fact that God "speaks to us" as individuals. It simply places everything within the proper framework: community. For example, in speaking to Moses, God spoke to the Israelite people; in speaking to Mary, God spoke to the Church; in speaking to the saints, God spoke to peoples everywhere for all time. To remain in our own little corner believing that we have single-handedly "discerned" God's Word is foolish and dangerous.

2. Decisions made during a life of discernment should always be consonant with the nature of the group or individual. In other words, we must stay within the proper sphere of our competency. It is self-defeating to decide something upon which we cannot act (leaving our family to become a monk in Tibet) while avoiding those very areas in which we can act (reading Scripture a half hour each day).

Implicit in this assumption is that decision-making in a life of discernment is something we do for ourselves—or for the group of which we are a part. We alone must choose the action we will take; others cannot decide for us. Lawful authority and tradition are present to confirm the validity of our choice by keeping us rooted in the community's experience; they are not present to remove decision-making from our lives. The input they offer is meant to clarify the choices possible, not to remove our freedom of choice.

Within the Church, and within its many movements of enthusiasm, e.g., charismatic renewal, marriage encounter, etc., there remains the danger of people's willingness to give up their responsibility to choose for themselves. This is done with all sincerity, believing that others (often those in authority) are meant to choose and decide for them. This is not meant to be. Tradition and lawful authority are called upon to help us decide properly, i.e., choose the Lord and his Kingdom in every situation. No one is meant to force that decision. To do so would be to take away the chance for growth which each choice and decision for the Lord usually bring.

Because of inadequate faith formation, many Christians are more comfortable when told what to do, rather than when encouraged to enter the life of discernment. The latter approach is hard work requiring prayer, fasting, etc., which prepares us to make decisions in light of the Spirit's movements within. The former asks only for blindness, which ignores the Light within.

This warning is given because discernment can be a weapon used by some to manipulate people. Do not believe that a "discerning person" is meant to tell us what to do. She/he may be called to clarify the situation for us so we can choose the Lord with more certainty. We, however, must choose to act for ourselves.

A good rule of thumb in this area is to keep all things in the light. Avoid following the directions of those unnamed groups (the "we" that nobody identifies) which state, "We've prayed and heard God say. . . ." In a similar vein, do not immediately follow the advice of an individual who manipulates with the words, "The Lord told me to tell you . . . ." Such absolute statements need testing against the criteria mentioned in previous chapters of this book.

3. The final assumption is the constant in the process of decision-making within the life of discernment: the glory of Jesus' cross will be revealed. Remember, however, that it is Jesus' cross which must be glorified—not our own self-imposed crosses. Very often, sincere Christians accept crosses which are not from the Lord. Many people automatically assume that any tragedy, heartbreak, or crisis

that might occur is from God, rather than seeing these experiences as part of our human condition. The Lord can and does use these situations, but they are not necessarily his cross, given so that God might be glorified. In deciding the validity of the cross in each situation, use selflessness as a sign. Does it call you to be selfless, and is it leading you to that reality with joy?

Legitimate Expectations in the Decision-Making Process

The Presence of the Risen Lord

The first and most important thing to expect is the Lord's presence. As we focus on those inner feelings or "spirits" which are part of our life in Jesus, we can expect the Lord to reveal his redeeming power and presence. This reality is of far greater importance than any specific answer we may be seeking. In fact, it is not unusual that the reality of the Lord's presence will be the only answer we receive while attempting to reach a decision in a difficult or confusing situation. Although we always hope for a clear choice, it may not be apparent at a given time. The Risen Lord, however, will always be apparent, if we are faithful in our life of discernment.

Healing and Forgiveness

Coupled with the power of the Risen Lord is his healing and forgiveness. Recall the section on interior freedom[1] which placed an emphasis upon the value of recognizing attitudes that need to be healed or forgiven, rather than on the importance of setting goals for ourselves. In seeking a specific decision, therefore, expect healing to occur both for ourselves and for others.

Forgiveness also will be present. We may be called to accept the Lord's forgiveness or to be his forgiveness for another. Should we create a barrier in these areas, clarity will not emerge and we will find it difficult to make a proper decision.

Wisdom and Prudence

Definitive answers (those true for all time) are never reached in the decision-making process of a life of discernment.[2] In fact, that which is *absolutely* best cannot be confirmed until we enter the Kingdom. What usually emerges during this intensified period of prayer and focusing is a "leaning towards" the Lord and his Kingdom. We lean towards the response we are best able to give at this time. Hopefully, tomorrow's "best" response will be better than today's "best" response.

Wisdom and prudence point out that our "leaning towards" the Kingdom might change in time depending on our "response-ability" and the grace of God. The Lord does not demand of us today what we can only do tomorrow.

Included in this assumption is the fact of our sinfulness: our human limitations which cannot be disregarded. Living the life of discernment does not free us from this fact. Only Jesus frees us. Discernment cannot remove from our lives the reality of our fear, our anger, our lack of freedom. Only Jesus does this. This freedom is accomplished over the span of our lifetime, through the process of spiritual growth and development.

Consolation and Desolation[3]

Think for a moment of an occasion when you felt the Lord's presence, when you experienced "moving with him." Now, jot down one-word descriptions of your feelings during this time. Do the same with an instance when you did not sense the Lord. If you can do this simple exercise, you will know the meaning of consolation and desolation.

Consolation comes as we move with God. The words normally associated with this experience are joy, peace, power, gentleness, etc. During a time of consolation there usually is an increase of faith, hope and love. With desolation, however, words such as anger, fear, unrest, anxiety, turmoil, etc., come to mind. In addition, we are not moved towards faith, hope and love.

In perceiving the difference between consolation and desolation, we become aware of God's input in the decision-making process of discernment; we can sense if God's Spirit is there, or if we are being led by a different "spirit." While reviewing the cons and pros of a possible decision, do we feel anxious or peaceful, joyful or fearful, etc.? This is the new data the Lord reveals to us, so that we might choose a response which leads towards him. A computer can methodically list pros and cons; only a person living a life of discernment, however, can recognize and interpret the consolation and desolation that touches his/her inner being.

As we grow deeper in the spiritual life, we will recognize these inner movements more easily. For example, we will notice how the promptings of a "good spirit" always bring courage, strength, inspiration and peace, whereas those of a "bad spirit" bring anxiety, doubts, sadness and false obstacles. In addition, a "good spirit" will affirm our name of grace and move us to remain faithful to God's call. A "bad spirit," however, destroys our inner integrity and wholeness, showing us only closed doors with no escape route.

Part of our task, therefore, in the decision-making process is to be conscious of these inner movements or feelings. Several questions which might enhance our awareness are listed for consideration.

1. How do I react when I feel angry (or joyful, etc.)?
2. What situations in my life trigger the above feeling?
3. What interior signs attract my attention before I respond to the above feelings?
4. How do I feel after I have acted on this feeling?

Journal keeping and a daily discernment examen will also assist in learning to recognize these signs of God's Spirit.

Three Examples by St. Ignatius[4]

St. Ignatius provides several graphic images[5] to help us anticipate the emergence of a "bad spirit" in our life of discernment.

One way to recognize a "bad spirit" is to imagine an angry person: frenzied, screaming, resentful, agitated. Such are the signs of a "bad spirit," of desolation, and like an angry person, they must be confronted with courage, lest they rule us against our will. To ignore the angry person does not make him/her go away; to ignore the signs of a "bad spirit" does not make it go away either.

A "bad spirit" is also like a false lover who secretly seduces his friend's daughter. Undoubtedly, the false lover would caution the daughter against sharing these encounters with her father. Secrecy, therefore, is a sign of a "bad spirit." It needs to be combated with openness. A spiritual director can help us to develop this openness by relating to us in love, so that we can keep all things in the light, thereby foiling the Evil One.

A third way to recognize a "bad spirit" is by thinking of an army general. In order to capture a city, he would circle about, looking for a vulnerable area. So with a "bad spirit" which will try to attack our area of vulnerability, whether it be pride, or misguided generosity, or laziness, or fear, etc. This is why self-knowledge is a critical factor in combating desolation. By knowing our strengths and weaknesses, we can be prepared for an attack, and not be caught off guard.

Prayer Exercise: Read Mark 10:23-31

—Begin with the usual preparatory prayer.

—Listen to the song, "Take, Lord, Receive"[6] which is based on a prayer by St. Ignatius.

—Do "Meditation on the Two Standards"[7] a paraphrase of which appears below:

Imagine the scene . . . a large field between two mountains. On either side of the field is an army, each carrying a banner or standard. In the center of the field stands a single person—you.

Look, now, toward one side. You recognize it as Satan's army. What does it look like? Satan, himself, sits enthroned on a seat that is red hot with fire and smoke. Try to imagine the harshness, the violence, the anger that emanates from his person. Then, look towards the other side. This army is different in appearance. They are not dressed for war but wear simple garb—they are defenseless and unarmed.

Standing in their midst is their King, Jesus the Lord: gentle, simple, attractive in appearance.

Suddenly, amidst cries of pain and shrieks of terror, Satan's army begins to move towards the center. Listen to the noise: the curses, the swearing, the rumble of angry people shoving and clawing their way forward. From the other side, however, comes a different sound: joy, psalms of praise, and cries of gladness arise as Jesus' army moves forward.

As each army approaches, notice the banners they carry. Can you see the words written on Satan's banner? Riches . . . Honor . . . Pride. Look now at Jesus' banner: Poverty . . . Insult . . . Humility. Both groups are moving closer; each army is calling out in full voice: "Come, you are mine. Come, you are mine. Come, you are mine."

Suddenly, you notice that you, too, are carrying a banner. Look at it. What does it say? Do you want to carry it, or are you going to thrust it aside because the words mockingly echo Satan's standards (perhaps your banner has lust, work, and manipulation written on it)? Do not despair, for in Jesus all things can be made new. Look again. The banner is blank; you are free to design your own standard. Choose your motto carefully, for the banner you carry indicates the army you have joined.

—Concluding Prayer

   —Ask Mary to obtain for you the grace needed to carry the standard of Jesus, first in the highest spiritual poverty, or actual poverty, if it be his pleasure; second, under the banner of insult and contempt; and, third, under the standard of humility.

   —Ask Jesus for the grace to be received under his banner. Ask the Lord to take your banner and change it to one of his.

   —Ask the Father for the above graces.

—Pray the Our Father.

—As a concluding song, listen to "I Lift Up My Soul,"[8] or a similar hymn.

A Contemporary Meditation on the Two Standards[9]

We do not need the gift of prophecy to realize that the world is in trouble. The media keeps us informed, with mind-numbing regularity, of each new world disaster. Our everyday conversations reveal the personal disasters we suffer. Crisis situations no longer surprise us. We feel, at times, like stunned observers of a holocaust, helpless and afraid.

We have gone through so many "emergencies": the energy crisis, the financial crisis, the hostage crisis, 9/11, a war in Iraq, heightened security. In addition, these have run parallel to other "disasters": the political crisis, the morality crisis, the nuclear crisis, and the sexual identity crisis. Problems seem to confront us at every turn. No wonder people think that the end is near; it could not possibly get worse! Or could it?

Our governments breed corruption, our cities breed pollution, while family after family succumbs to the social diseases of anxiety and depression. The poor in our midst remain poor; the elderly grow not only in age but in fear. We who are called to be stewards of God's creation, exploit and rape what God has created.

Nothing seems to work. We have gone through the New Deal, the Fair Deal, the New Society, and the Great Society. Yet, such programs have done nothing more than reveal the depth of poverty and decay that is present. We have gone through wars which were to end all war and built bombs which would halt further bombings. In reality, however, we have caused the death of millions because money was spent on arms rather than on people.

Within our very soul we sense this decay. Sexual values and norms, for example, have reached a nadir as seen so graphically on commercial billboards that line our highways: ads that shout "want," "more," "better," "fulfill me," "now." Self-gratification has replaced love and commitment in the same way that the god of military superiority and consumerism has replaced the God of the peacemaker and the poor.

Even our churches bear the rotten fruit sown throughout the world—bishops covering up wrongdoing, clergy abuse of children, Church leaders resigning and/or being prosecuted by state law enforcers—despite the pockets of renewal which struggle to survive. Multinational corporations are not the only large enterprises that seek power and control over people's lives. For example, in our own communities we see the clergy, parish leaders, and many others seeking to control and manipulate through a misuse of authority and a misunderstanding of the Law of Love.

We need not pray for a prophetic vision to "see" these things; they are already obvious. In fact, they are so prevalent we have grown numb, lest we live on the edge of total despair. We have learned to cope by nodding our agreement, by saying, "Yes, it really is terrible. But what can be done?" We have convinced ourselves we are enlightened when, in reality, we stumble about in the dark.

This, then is the question: "Is this the world which God intended? Is this the same world which the Book of Genesis called good? Is the world about us, with its perversion and poverty, its anger and violence, the same world which Jesus made new by his death on the cross?

No! Jesus did not die on the cross so millions could remain hungry and chained by poverty. Jesus did not die on the cross so that children could live on drugs and women destroy the life within their wombs through abortions. Jesus died on the cross so that we could experience the real world—the world of his Father, the Kingdom come in our midst, the world touched by his redeeming blood!

The world we know is not that world created and redeemed by God and called "good" in the Bible. The world we experience now is a make-believe world, created by selfishness and pride—our own little "magic kingdom," without the magic. Today's world claims violence and anger, murder and hate, sloth and greed as its permanent denizens. By cautioning us to be in the world but not of it, John's Gospel tells us to live in the real world created and redeemed by Jesus (see Jn 17); to reject the make-believe world which we ourselves have created.

In his books, *The Chronicles of Narnia*, the very wise Christian author, C.S. Lewis, shows us what it means to live in the real world. The heroine, Lucy, learns from her friend, Aslan—a lion, who most believe represents Jesus—that she and her companions have chosen a wrong direction for their journey. Only Lucy sees and hears Aslan at this point in the story. Upon seeing Aslan, she immediately tells her companions. Deciding, however, not to follow her advice because they did not see Aslan themselves, her fellow travelers continue on their own way, encountering many difficulties and hardships. Eventually, they lose ground in their attempt to advance. Weary and exhausted, they fall asleep. Suddenly, "Lucy woke out of the deepest sleep you can imagine, with the feeling that the voice she liked best in the world had been calling her name." Responding to that voice, she hurries into the forest and finds Aslan. Putting her arms around him, she cries. "I saw you all right. They wouldn't believe me. . . . From somewhere deep inside Aslan's body there came the faintest suggestion of a growl. . . . The Lion looked straight into her eyes. 'Oh, Aslan, . . . I couldn't have left the others and come up to you alone, how could I? . . . oh well, I suppose I *could*. Yes, and it wouldn't have been alone, I know, not if I was with you.' "[10]

We are called to live in the world Jesus created and redeemed. The fact that others do not choose to follow should not deter us from our course. We must choose again and again to live in the real world of the Father's forgiveness and love, the real world of the Spirit's power and counsel, the real world of the Lord's Kingdom. Unfortunately, our society attempts to convince us that its own artificial world is the best possible one. This is not to be believed. The world our society has created is not built on Christ: its foundation is pride, greed and lust. This so-called world has little to do with the Lord, whose creation is built on love of neighbor and service to others.

Jesus died on the cross to reveal the deepest and most profound truth: God's infinite love for us. Outside of that truth there is nothing; outside of that reality there exists a self-constructed myth devoid of life and breath. Outside of that reality is death.

How can we recognize this truth? In answering that question we must look to the saints. One of the most outstanding is St. Francis of Assisi, a poor man who lived simply, sharing everything he had. He was a man in touch with his God, a man who communicated freely with the One Who created him. In addition, he was a man who, tradition tells us, conversed also with God's creation. He talked to the animals and called the sun his brother, the moon, his sister. Today, we might look upon this as a story of doubtful authenticity. Yet, in Jesus' world, nothing is impossible. Just because we, who do not live in the real world, cannot talk to animals, does not mean that St. Francis (who lived in the real world) did not. In fact, we might even say that when we enter the real world of Jesus as deeply as St. Francis did, we too will indeed talk to the animals!

Ignatius of Loyola is another remarkably inspiring saint. He was a soldier who gave up everything to become powerless in the presence of God; a cripple who walked with grace through the real world revealed to him in Jesus; a proud person who learned submission and love. He was a saint then and today, one from whom we might learn the ways of the Kingdom.

Think of Mary: simple, trusting, open. She lived in the real world, the world where the Father spoke to His children, the world where the Lord was vibrantly alive, where the Spirit dwelled. So completely did she try to live in God's creation, that God Himself accepted her womb as His world through the Incarnation.

A saint in our own lifetime was Blessed Mother Teresa of India. She was an elderly woman— vibrant, alive in God, poor and holy—who cared for the sick and dying in the streets of Calcutta. There, amidst the worst slum imaginable, with a stench that would drive us back to our airplanes, there in that filth, Blessed Mother Teresa lived in the real world; she lived in Jesus' world. After spending her morning in prayer before the Blessed Sacrament, she went into the streets and brought the dying back to her home where they may die with dignity and peace. We called it heroic and offered her medals; she called it normal and offered her life. She lived in the real world.

What about ourselves? How can we take up residence in the real world of Jesus Christ crucified and raised from the dead? First we must acknowledge the existence of two worlds;[11] we must acknowledge that conflict exists within our culture, and society is telling us a lie. By ignoring this situation, we remain deceived, always believing that glass is diamond, that tin is gold, that scrap is banquet. By ignoring this reality we remain prey to the intent of the Evil One, who would deceive us with his lies.

His plan of attack ignores no one. He craves control over all people—rich and poor alike. He begins by convincing us to acquire riches, by tempting us to accumulate wealth of any type in order to be assured of salvation in a crumbling world. In addition, we are told that this accumulation will bring us honor. The honor attained, of course, is empty, but it is the honor recognized by the world: a larger car, a better school, a second home, etc. As these so-called honors increase, we become bloated with pride, which is the most difficult chain to cast off. In three easy steps—riches, honor, pride—we are then led to every other vice. For example, our pride leads to violence because we must defend our riches; this leads to ruthlessness because we must defend our honor, etc.

The plan of Jesus, however, is radically different. He also overlooks no one and speaks his saving gospel to all. First, however, he invites us to embrace the highest spiritual poverty, and if we are lucky, invites us to embrace actual poverty. In accepting his invitation, we do not receive accolades and honor, but scorn and contempt. We are called to wear them joyfully because they lead to humility, and when we are humble, we embody the Gospel.

This may not sound very appealing. In fact, our society tells us that such a plan of action is sheer madness. We must not forget, however, the proof of its validity: the resurrection of Jesus from the dead.

When we celebrate the sacraments, we touch the real world of Jesus—the world of true reality. This is especially true of the Eucharist, wherein we claim the Body and Blood of the Lord as our true center, wherein we claim, with certainty, that Jesus is alive in our midst!

---

[1] Chapter Four, Tool #5.

[2] Even when "discerning" the sacrament of marriage, for example, the Church acknowledges that the discernment may have been skewed by a lack of data. The annulment process shows how a marriage which is presupposed as being forever can be reevaluated based on previously unknown data.

[3] *The Spiritual Exercises of St. Ignatius,* translated by Louis J. Puhl (Chicago, IL: Loyola University Press, 1951), Sections 322-324.

[4] Sections 325-327 in the *Exercises.*

[5] Some of Ignatius' images convey an unacceptable stereotype to contemporary sensibilities. I have altered them slightly since his culturally bound and shaped examples are not intrinsic to his point.

[6] Taken from "Earthen Vessels," by the St. Louis Jesuits. Published and distributed by Oregon Catholic Press. Phone: 1-800-LITURGY.

[7] A standard is a medieval banner which is designed to represent a particular group, guild, or town, etc. See 136-148 in *Exercises.*

[8] Taken from, "A Dwelling Place," by the St Louis Jesuits. Published and distributed by Oregon Catholic Press. Phone: 1-800-LITURGY.

[9] This "meditation" is offered as a further point of reflection.

[10] C.S. Lewis, *Prince Caspian* (New York: The Macmillan Company, 1951), 113-118.

[11] I am not proposing here a dualistic world view or a Platonist stance toward reality. The example is simply stated to assist the imagination in the meditative process.

Chapter 6

The Process

The following steps outline the process of decision-making that emerges with a life of discernment.

1. *Prayer*. The process of decision-making begins with prayer. St. Ignatius urges us to be specific, begging again and again for light and purification. Although the light may seem blinding at first, although the stripping may seem painful, we need these two graces, if we are to enter the decision-making process properly. This first step is ongoing. One does not simply pray a Hail Mary and proceed to the other steps. It presupposes an ongoing prayer time with the Lord.

2. *Formulation of the Proposition*. As we pray for interior freedom, we can begin to formulate our proposition. It should concern an important and real matter which is presently at hand. Avoid speculations and intellectualizations. Topics for our proposition can cover any area of our life: Should we change our job? Should we work with the elderly? Should we schedule a "hermit" day every month for prayerful meditation and reflection, etc.?

In forming the proposition, make a clear, concise and affirmative statement. Commit that statement to writing. As an example, we will use the following proposition: "I propose to spend two hours every Wednesday afternoon to work in the parish's food pantry." A poorly phrased proposition would be less specific and lack clarity, e.g., "I propose to volunteer more time to serve the poor." When beginning to write, therefore, always ask the "how to's," such as when, where, how, how long, with whom, why, etc.

3. *Gather the Data.* Once we formulate the proposition, begin to gather all the information needed to make a wise and prudent decision. To gather the information for the above proposition, the following questions might be asked: How will I get there? Who will take care of the baby? Will my family approve? Will the pantry be open? What will I do during the time in the pantry? When will I begin? What hours will I be absent from home, etc.?

4. *Cons and Pros.* Once the data is gathered, move towards times of intensified prayer, asking, as always, for the specific graces needed to make a proper decision. Then, looking at the information gathered and the proposition formulated, list all the cons, i.e., the reasons why we should not follow this particular proposition. Compose this list while in prayer; taking as long as needed, using as many prayer periods as we feel are necessary.

As the cons emerge from our inner self, write them down. Once completed, do the same for the pros, listing all the reasons for acting upon the proposition. Experience has shown it best to list the cons first, in order to let the pros emerge freely.

How long should this process take? It depends upon each situation. Expecting God to speak within a certain period of time is presumption; deciding to stop after a certain period of time might be good planning!

5. *Sifting and condensing.* After the cons and pros are listed, begin to separate them according to their order of importance. Weigh each con carefully, realizing that some are more important than others. For example, the fact that we might have to change our laundry day is not as important a consideration as having to leave our baby with a sitter for a period of time.

After sifting the cons, proceed to the pros. Eliminate duplication and condense the lists.

6. *Prayer.* Having come this far, continue to ask God's blessing, praying for light and purification. Persevering in prayer, we now inspect our lists, noting what we feel as we reflect on the cons and then the pros. We are looking here for experiences of consolation and/or desolation—those inner movements which indicate the Lord's presence. In noting these inner movements, we will have a better idea of the Lord's presence in the situation being considered.

7. *Decision to Act.* Once that "sense" is acknowledged, we should choose to act, since it is in our response that we will find the Lord. Remember that a decision to change our course of action should never be made during the feeling of desolation, since that would indicate that the Lord is not present.

After making our choice, pray with diligence that the Lord will confirm this choice, if it is for his greater service and glory. The making of a decision, however, does not eliminate the need for continued humility, for seeking the graces needed to fulfill the choice.

How will God confirm our choice? Through experiences of peace and inner joy. For example, in the case of our test proposition, we would find that our time working in the food pantry energizes us. Most especially, however, God confirms our choice through an increased desire and ability to die to self, as we serve others in love.

Decision-Making in a Community—Some Observations

The process of communal decision-making remains basically the same. As with individual decision-making, the formulation of the proposition is very important. It needs to be specific and affirmative. The gathering of data is also quite similar. Now, however, a group of people, rather than simply an individual, is called upon to share its input. In doing so, each individual should strive to uncover all the necessary data, the "how to's." All possible evidence should be given and clarified, keeping everything in the light. There will be times, of course, when some data cannot be revealed (e.g., items under the seal of confession), but those times are the exception rather than the norm. Holding back available data because we did not think it was important detracts from the chances of truly choosing the Lord in the situation at hand.

Additional data is gathered after each individual has listed his/her cons and pros. Remember that this initial listing should be done individually without consultation or discussion with others. After each person has made a list, that list is shared—beginning with the cons—by stating clearly and simply what each person feels the Lord is telling him/her to do. Each person in turn, therefore, is asked to share one con until all the cons are shared. Should an individual finish his/her list before the others he/she would simply pass, until all the cons are shared.

The same is done for the pros. Each person has the responsibility to speak since this sharing is the new data available—data given to each person in prayer, hence, data which may be from the Spirit of God.

In sharing this new data (i.e., the sharing of the cons and pros), avoid debate and argument. In proceeding from one person to another, simply state, "I feel the Lord is telling us 'no' (or 'yes') because . . . ." Then state one reason and let the next person share. Do not state all your reasons at once lest a person does not share because one individual has dominated.

Such a process takes quite a bit of time. With large groups it can become tedious, although variations of the method have been used.[1] The process, however, will bear fruit if we see it through.

Once the additional data is given, each individual takes his/her list, eliminates duplication, and continues the process at Step Five, that of sifting and condensing.

When it is time for the group to make a decision, they should gather in prayer and state, one at a time, "I feel the Lord is asking us to follow (or not follow) the proposition." There is no discussion at this time, no reasons are given other than each one's personal sense of where the Lord is leading. Once each person has shared, the group will probably discover that the Lord has peacefully leaned everyone's heart in a similar direction.

The Need for Consensus

In trying to make decisions with others, keep in mind that the fastest runners—we might call them prophets, those who see beyond the mountain—may sometimes need to slow down, so that the rest of the group can build up endurance for the journey. This does not mean that an individual should refrain from speaking the Lord's word within the decision-making process. St. Francis of Assisi is a good example. He needed to grow in patience with his small community, often "compromising" because the group's "response-ability" was less than his own. Yet, interiorly he took giant steps toward spiritual fulfillment growing in wisdom, prudence and wholeness. Should an individual in a group find his/her "discernment" over-ruled, the individual should continue to seek the Lord by dying to self in the present situation so that a new dawn might emerge tomorrow.

This does not mean that any individual within a group is meant to go against conscience, lawful authority, Scripture, church teaching, etc. Those are the very para-meters within which the group's decision-making process must remain. It does mean, however, that each person strives to accept the limitations of others, taking care not to push others forward, but to love them forward, one step at a time, in seeking the Lord.

For example, in the initial stages of St. Ignatius' experi-ence, while he and his disciples were deciding on the structure of their society, they all agreed to a particular plan of action. In subsequent decisions they always reached consensus. The time eventually came, however, when consensus, their anticipated unanimity, was not reached. It was then that they realized that they could still make a decision although consensus had not been pre-sent. Avoid, therefore, carrying unnecessary burdens such as waiting for what is not needed.

Should consensus be reached during the decision-making process, thank the Lord. Should there remain an element of dissent, remember that sometimes to disagree is to be catholic! Consensus may be God's gift to a group; it may however, stem from our desire to conform. We might all agree because we lack interior freedom, when in reality God wanted some to disagree in order to keep the door open for further growth.

Signs of a Spirit-filled Decision

With both individual and/or communal decision-making, expect to experience the usual signs: internal joy, interior freedom, peace, etc. If these feelings are lacking, reexamine the process.

Even when a community lacks consensus, peace usually will be present if the Spirit of God is being followed, if we are striving to choose the Lord as sincerely as we are able at the time of choice. In such cases, decisions coming from the Lord usually build community, while decisions arising from our human spirits usually destroy community. Lack of consensus, therefore, does not imply God is not leading. The dissenting voice may in itself be part of the process and plan of God. Saints Paul, Joan of Arc, Teresa of Avila, et. al., are examples of men and women whose dissenting voices became the call to tomorrow's dawn. This can occur because consensus alone is not the sign of God's leading; it is not what makes a community one. Charity, which covers a multitude of sins and limitations, is the bond which brings oneness and points to the Lord.

In making a communal choice, therefore, remember that we are called in love to carry each other's burdens, the heaviest being the imperfect judgments and half-hearted responses each of us makes when seeking the Lord.

Obstacles to Discernment[2]

Throughout the time of decision-making in our life of discernment, expect to encounter the obstacles of Untruth and Unfreedom.

Untruth (Darkness of Mind)

Into this category falls any kind of darkness in our life: our human limitations, lack of knowledge, ignorance of the facts, or our inability to collect all the data needed to make a good decision. Very often we are not responsible for these obstacles, yet they are part of our present reality.

A common example of this darkness would be our lack of self-knowledge or our poor self-image. Think of the times when we accepted the false definitions thrust upon us by an unbelieving and unloving world: "God can't love me because I'm so rotten" or "I can't do that, I never do anything right." Such slogans bend us out of shape, keeping us locked in darkness and untruth. To break free, we must seek the graces of interior freedom mentioned in the previous chapter.

A basic untruth which stymies the decision-making process is our assumption that a person's goodwill and sincerity automatically remove all barriers. Unfortunately, this is not so. A sincere person may sound quite impressive, but she/he may be sincerely wrong, and may be leading in the wrong direction. Truth is needed in addition to sincerity and honesty. Truth alone prepares the correct path upon which we can walk towards the Lord.

Unfreedoms (Darkness of Will)

Fear is, perhaps, the most debilitating unfreedom which plagues our life. It paralyzes us, making us immobile, tense and anxious. We fear making mistakes and displeasing our peers. We fear disappointment, suffering, and sometimes even love. We fear God's call and what God might ask of us. We fear the radical call of the Gospel, and sometimes we even fear ourselves.

Mixed with this fear is prejudice—our unwillingness to change and/or be changed. Too often, we limit our use of the word prejudice to racial relationships when, more frequently, it can be used to describe our lack of openness to deeper truths. The way to recognize prejudice is to look for the always/never statement. For example, "The Mass can't be in English because it has always been in Latin" or "Black people never hold a job for long periods of time." This is prejudice at its core: a failure to touch the deeper truth.

Other obstacles to discernment are our unrealistic expectations and assumptions. For example, we expect the Lord to speak to us, so we pray for a moment and then open the Bible in order to hear God's Word. This type of Bible bingo carries with it unrealistic expectations. Or, perhaps, our prayer has been dry over the past few weeks, so we assume that God is leading us away from prayer! An unrealistic assumption to say the least.

A common obstacle, one that stems from our misguided sense of prudence, is indecision. By holding off a deci-

sion until we are "absolutely certain," we are really deciding not to decide. To feel reasonably assured and to move
in faith is generally all that is necessary if we are going to
lean toward the Lord. Remember also, we are not deciding infallibly. Discernment does not make that boast.

Finally, under the guise of being open to the Lord we
often erect the obstacle called passivity. "I'll just pray"
sums up this attitude. This is a type of misguided openness wherein we refuse to take any initiative, just in case
God wants to do something else. On the other side of this
coin is the person whose openness is really a caving in to
inner compulsiveness and desires. This type of misguided openness is a barrier to our hearing, seeing and listening to the Lord.

Take consolation in knowing that such obstacles are
part of normal, spiritual growth We should not think that
we have been singled out for punishment or for attack by
the Evil One. They are merely opportunities for us to
encounter, in our response, the converting and transform-
ing power of Christ.

Tactics to Combat the Obstacles[3]

Prayer

Faithfulness to solitary prayer helps us to stop, look
and listen. Such prayer leads us to see the nothingness
and lifelessness that exists without the Lord. All forms of
prayer are helpful: the petition for interior freedom, the
quiet contemplation of Gospel truths, worship and praise
through song and tongues, the stillness of centering on
God within, etc.

Asceticism

Acts of asceticism are another weapon in overcoming the obstacles to discernment. Basic, physical acts such as fasting will put us in touch with the deepest reality dwelling within, keeping us ever mindful that Jesus alone is the food that satisfies all hunger. Sleeping on the floor, celibacy, and other purely physical disciplines are part of this ascetical arsenal. Be careful, however, lest we follow a wrong spirit. Submission to a spiritual guide rooted in Church tradition is a recommended precaution. Such a guide will help us avoid the pious enthusiasm which easily creeps into our spiritual life patterns.

There are other types of asceticism. Psychological asceticism, for example, will teach us how to recognize our fantasies and perceive the areas of our life which need healing. Do we know how to deal with destructive thoughts or accusations? Do we imagine a full scenario ending with righteous triumph over a person who has harmed us? How to handle such thoughts is the fruit of psychological asceticism.

Almsgiving, Bible reading, retreats, etc., are types of spiritual asceticism which nourish our inner self, thereby strengthening our ability to overcome the obstacles which surround us. Use all these weapons in the battle for purity of heart as you seek the Lord in the decision-making process.

Prayer Exercise

Choose some matter about which a decision is due and formulate a proposition. Keep the statement simple, clear and positively expressed. If necessary, divide it into two separate propositions for the sake of clarity. The discernment which follows should provide a "yes" or "no" answer to the proposition.

Meditation Poem: "I Lifted My Eyes"

As an opening prayer, you might find the following set of verses helpful.

> I lifted my eyes to the mountain up above,
> and I saw upon the mountain the Savior—he is Love.
> So I left my things behind for he said to travel light,
> and he took me by the hand ever upward through the
>   night.
> The climb's been long and hard, yet he's never let me
>   go;
> and he tells me everyday all the things I should know.
> The journey still goes on for my trust must still increase
> if I ever mean to rest forever in his peace.
> I lifted my eyes to the mountain up above,
> and I saw upon the mountain the Savior. He is Love.[4]

---

[1] Working with smaller groupings within the larger group is a possibility. Religious orders have learned a great deal in this regard from their experiences of chapter meetings.

[2] Taken from notes distributed at the Jesuit Center for Spiritual Growth, Wernersville, PA.

[3] *Ibid.*

[4] Copyright 1975 by C. Aridas.

Chapter 7

Checking Inner Attitudes

Heavenly Father,
we ask that you place within our hearts
the grace of perseverance,
the grace of long-suffering and patience,
so that our lives may remain focused
on the saving message of your Son, Jesus.
Help us to look neither to the left nor the right,
but to him who is our source of life and hope.

At this point, we need to observe more carefully what is happening inside our hearts. Having formulated a proposition and gone through the cons and pros, we may be experiencing a "what's next" type of feeling. Perhaps we are having some difficulty trying to figure out what the Lord wants, even though we've already considered the obstacles presented in the last chapter.

Should this be the case, it is time to reassess our intention, to be sure we are seeking *the proper end result,* i.e., seeking union with God. If we are having difficulty in making a choice, it is quite possible that we have not chosen the proper end. Perhaps we are making a means the end. For example, many choose to serve God through marriage (although the service of God is the end). The proper intention is to serve God and then, choose marriage as a means to that end. Some might choose a school or a job in the same fashion, substituting the means for the end.

This distinction is difficult to make because our entire society urges us to choose school, job, spouse, etc., as ends in themselves, rather than first to choose God and let all other choices support this ultimate good. In choosing, therefore, we must make sure that our intention is correct: are we seeking God through a particular choice?

Another reason we may experience difficulty might be that we are not dealing with an important matter or that we are dealing with a subject beyond our competence. The decision-making process will bear fruit only if the subject at hand is good or neutral. For example, we should not "employ" the decision-making process in order to ask the Lord whether we should continue an adulterous relationship. Nor should we use this method if the proposition is dealing with an unchangeable situation e.g., a marriage which had been validly contracted with faith and interior freedom.[1]

Perhaps our difficulty in choosing stems from the fact that we have already chosen correctly in this matter, hence our efforts are redundant. Should there be doubt as to the correctness of our choice, then the process can be continued.

Sometimes it happens that a correct choice is made for the wrong reasons. When we discover this, it is wise to choose again so that our response to God is for the right reasons. For example, in entering the seminary to study for the priesthood, I chose that vocation for the wrong reasons. I was substituting the means (becoming a priest) for the end (serving God). It was only after three years that I realized how my initial choice was based on wrong reasons. Therefore, I had to re-choose my vocation for the right reasons.

Once a decision has been reached, remember that the process merely shows us how to "lean towards" the Kingdom. Because of our sinfulness and our human limitations, there is always some lack of interior freedom present when we choose. Even after choosing, we need to allow ourselves time to discover what further purifications need to be made.

St. Ignatius gives several helpful images which can assist us in the process of choosing:[2]

1. When the time comes for a choice to be made, having looked at the cons and the pros, and having sifted through and articulated the spirits of consolation and desolation, imagine a person you do not know. What choice would you encourage that person to make for the greater glory of God and the perfection of his/her soul? You should do likewise.

2. Imagine you are at the point of death. What course of action would you wish to have followed if you could relive the moment? You, then, should now choose that course.

3. Let us now picture ourselves before the Lord of Judgment. Reflect on what decision you wish you had made regarding the proposition presently at hand. This is the decision you should make now.

Three Types of Humility[3]

A crucial interior disposition in the decision-making process, one which requires our regular attention, is expressed by the word humility.

The first and most basic type of humility is that which is necessary for salvation. The person who is humble in this way is willing to be subject to the law of God, and resolves never to disobey that law even if it means death. For this person, mortal sin would never be chosen even if threatened with death.

The second type of humility is more perfect than the first. The person possessing this humility neither desires nor is inclined to have riches rather than poverty, or to seek honor rather than dishonor, or to desire a long life rather than a short one. In short, such a person is detached; she/he is not prone to either alternative except to the degree that it helps her/him serve God and allows a dying to self. In addition to these characteristics, the second type of humility also includes a willingness or a resolve not to commit any type of sin: if there were a choice between losing her/his life or committing a venial sin[4] she/he would forfeit life. For example, one might be given the opportunity to advance in business through dishonest means. Humility of the second type would repudiate such a choice.

The third and most perfect type of humility presupposes the first two and then, whenever the glory and praise of God would be equally served, chooses to imitate Christ the Lord.

Choose poverty with Christ rather than riches; choose insult with Christ crucified rather than honor; choose to be counted worthless and a fool for Christ, rather than to be esteemed wise by this world's standards. This third type of humility hearkens back to the meditation on the two standards.

If we are having difficulty making a choice, we may be lacking the proper degree of humility. Does this mean that the third type of humility is needed to make a perfect choice? Yes, that is exactly what it means. Does this mean we cannot make a choice without that type of humility? No, rather it means that we are to choose in the best way possible at the moment; it means we should present ourselves in the best way possible in the "now." The Lord always accepts this offering. Do not be tricked into thinking that we must attain step three before making a choice.

A final difficulty in choosing is often seen in our refusal to use the ordinary, Christian means of detaching ourselves from self, i.e., we avoid the "Christ Crucified for the service of others" criterion, described previously. Experience shows us that decisions are more difficult to make if we are afraid to pay the price. This is evidenced by our hope that God will come into our desire, rather than deciding to give up our desire to come into God.

We combat these interior dispositions by prayer. St. Ignatius urges us to pray specifically for the grace to embrace that direction which repels us. If, therefore, we are uncomfortable with a certain type of humility or poverty, pray that our hearts will embrace it; pray for the courage and wisdom to accept these graces when they are given to us.

Such an approach is not meant to be a type of Christian masochism that advocates pain because pain is good.

Sentimental piety might hold that notion. On the contrary, we are simply advocating the acceptance of Christ's banner, even when uncomfortable. This is a lifetime process wherein we play for keeps. It is not a mental exercise that may or may not work. It is forever. In the context of eternity then, remember that the Love of God is our very life; and His love is forever.

Meditation Poem: "Your Love's Forever"

To live with all the sorrows that we bear is not easy.
'Cause living in a land that's dry to dreams leaves us
    empty.
And we're getting nowhere fast,
hindered by our wounded past
till we call your name at last.
Your love's forever. Your peace endures.
If we stay here in Your name we'll feel secure.
You hear us crying our silent tears.
So we stay as close as fear will let you near.
To hear each other's constant cries of pain makes us
    weary.
And bleeding while we dress another's wounds, leaves
    us lonely.
Feeling hollow, feeling used,
we're exhausted and confused.
Still we reach for what is true.
Your love's forever.[5]

---

[1] St. Ignatius points out that some "unchangeable" decisions lacked true interior freedom when the choice was made. Such decisions should be re-worked within the decision-making process. A vocation choice, not freely made, is not really a vocation or call from God. A perverse choice is never a divine choice. Cf. section 172 in *Exercises*.
[2] Cf. sections 185-187 in *Exercises*.

[3] Cf. Sections 165-167 in *Exercises*.

[4] It is important for us to understand correctly the notion of sin. We must remember that the words, "mortal" and "venial" are simply word-constructs used to describe a degree of movement away from God. Be careful to remember, however, that any movement away from God is not desirable. Too often, we think that "venial" sins are okay, while "mortal" sins must be avoided. Avoid the semantics of saying "I've only committed a venial sin." What this really means is that we have damaged our relationship with Life itself. Imagine a scuba diver whose air hose gets more and more narrow. Eventually, air will no longer reach the diver and his life will be in jeopardy. Venial sin has a similar effect on our souls.

[5] Copyright 1980, William Boecker.

Chapter 8

Day by Day[1]

Let's begin with a story: "While living in the palace, Abba Arsenius prayed to God in these words: 'Lord, lead me in the way to salvation.' And a voice came to him saying, 'Arsenius, flee from the world and you will be saved.' Having sailed secretly from Rome to Alexandria and having withdrawn to the solitary life in the desert, Arsenius prayed again: 'Lord, lead me in the way of salvation,' and again he heard a voice saying, 'Arsenius, flee, be silent, pray always, for these are the source of sinlessness.' "[2]

There are three key words for reflection: flee (seek solitude), be silent, pray always. Through the proper integration of those inner attitudes, we will discover a life in the Spirit, which means we will discover our life of discernment. At first glance, these words might imply an other worldly spirituality that cannot exist in our modern society. In fact, however, a desert spirituality nurtured by these three words must become our own spirituality lest modern society squeeze us into non-existence.

Solitude

A recurring word in spiritual life and growth is solitude. Despite its importance throughout our churches' experience, however, we continue to ignore its call. The fact, nonetheless, remains: passively drifting along, accepting the busy-ness of our society, propels us to ruin. Despite our wishing the contrary, our society is not aglow with Christ's love. We may wish it were so, but it is not. One does not have to embrace a "world is evil" framework to acknowledge the obvious: that our society fosters and supports a dominating and manipulating spirit which easily strangles and crushes believers. In response to this, we, the children of light, quickly conspire with the darkness. We join the "children of darkness" on their own turf, playing the game with their rules, when, in reality, we should flee and seek solitude.

This is not meant as a condemnation, but as a simple observation. Let's look at our agendas, at our plans for tomorrow. Are we planning a time for prayer and praise? Are we questioning our activities as to their worth and priority? Probably not. We seldom ask such questions, and seldom try to answer them! More than likely, our tomorrow is already planned for us, and we simply hope that with our "extra time" we will be able to do those things we know are important. Seldom do we look to see if our activity during the day nourishes us. We usually assume that certain things must be done or ought to be done. This approach bears little fruit.

Such an attitude in our day-to-day routine gives us the first reason we lack solitude in our life: our mistaken self-identity. We usually rely on our society to define us, to tell us who we are and what is expected of us. Very likely, we want to measure up to those expectations, lest others speak or think ill of us. Our society does not expect us to seek solitude, hence, our moving in that direction threatens our very self-identity. Yet, as mentioned previously, our real self-identity comes from God, not from society. To ignore the call for solitude is to accept a mistaken self-identity, a self-definition not rooted in the Lord.

A second impediment to our seeking solitude is our fear of what we will find. No one wants to be alone, only to discover the inner spirits of anger, lust, pride and greed moving ferociously within. Better to keep busy than to acknowledge the existence of such spirits; better to avoid solitude completely by sitting back and doing what we want rather than sitting still and doing what God wants. Such an attitude will not lead us to the place of solitude which we are encouraged to seek.

For the Desert Fathers, and for us, solitude is a place of transformation and conversion; a place where we are weak, vulnerable and naked; a place where there are no supports giving us a false self-identity. In the beginning, solitude is a place of great discomfort where we are forced to meet and fight the enemies within: anger, lust, greed, pride, etc. We have seen these enemies before—denizens of our contemporary society, which has found them acceptable. When we discover them within, however, they become unbearable, forcing us to fight or be defeated. This vital process takes place in solitude.

Solitude is the place where we struggle with our confusions and our fantasies, our self-indulgent dreams of power and wealth. In solitude, we discover the truth of our relationships and the reality of our self-deceptions. Solitude is where battles are fought and battle scars won. Yet, who wants to do battle and become scarred? And so we do not seek a place of solitude because of fear.

Experience has shown the community of believers, however, that this encounter must not be avoided: we must discover the enemy within and enter into the struggle with him/her (the "him/her," of course, being our self), bearing at all times the Lord's standard and weapons; fighting with boldness and faith the false self so that the new self may emerge. This takes place in solitude.

It is essential, therefore, that we set time aside each day to be alone with the Lord, in this place of conversion and transformation. By avoiding such times, we become victims of a society which hides our true identity in the lies of its anger and greed. By embracing such times, however, we embrace the very place where the Lord Jesus reminds us that we are loved beyond all imagining. So, like the Desert Fathers, we must flee to our desert place of solitude.

Silence

What should we look for in this solitude? Silence: the practical way in which solitude becomes a reality. Silence: our portable desert which allows us a place of solitude even amidst others. Silence: the quietness of heart which avoids words so we might encounter God's Word. Through the practical discipline of silence, we remain in touch with Jesus' world, his Kingdom, while preserving ourselves from the worries, cares, and anxieties that our society has woven into its very fabric. As is said in Proverbs 10:19, "A flood of words is never without fault."

The Desert Fathers knew the importance of silence. They realized that useless words and conversations sapped their strength, making them citizens of society rather than citizens of the Kingdom. Think of personal experiences and conversations which were mindless, numbing, discouraging, inane; conversations which said nothing and drained us of joy and peace in the process. Silence protects us from such experiences.

A further reason for silence is to guard the God within, to guard the life of the Spirit. For example, automatic and/or non-reflective faithsharing may be led by a spirit of compulsiveness rather than the Spirit of Jesus. Our task is to make sure that we do not allow our inner energy to dissipate unnecessarily. Better to say a little than a lot, allowing a reflective, inner silence determine the words we choose. Always keep in mind that a verbal stream of consciousness is not faithsharing.

In silence, we learn how to speak, because a word with power is a word nurtured in silence—the divine silence in which love and forgiveness rest secure. Remember also, that silence of the heart is more important than silence of the tongue. We would be foolish to think a lack of spoken words indicated a growth in the Spirit, when our heart remained full of wordless gossip and slander. We are seeking a heart-felt silence which embraces the mystery of God's presence in and among us.

Prayer

There is little sense seeking solitude, little sense being silent, if we are not praying. The hermits and monks of our churches do not seek solitude and embrace silence for any reason other than their desire to converse with the Word, Jesus, who emerges in silence. They move from solitude to silence for prayer.

While solitude, for the Desert Fathers, was being alone with God, praying was their presence to God. In thinking of the exhortation, "Pray always," think first of its Greek root which means, "Come to rest." Praying is our resting in God in the midst of temptation, struggle and pain. It is a resting in God sought at all costs—even when the body is restless, or the world lures us elsewhere, or our inner spirits remain apathetic.

In praying always, we are not called to speak a prayer solely of the mind. It is not simply the activity of speaking with or thinking pleasant thoughts about God. Prayer is also a speaking that springs from the heart in wordless phrases. For example, there are no words which can fully convey the feelings of love and concern we feel for our family. The same is true with God, which is why a silent, wordless prayer is acceptable.

By entering into such a prayer, we are challenged to surrender ourselves to the Lord, we are challenged to hide nothing from Him. Such a prayer unmasks our illusions and false notions about ourselves, helping us to enter into the proper relationship of child to Father. Such a prayer is the prayer of truth and total rest: "I hold myself in quiet and silence, like a child in its mother's arms" (Ps 131:2). This is the prayer of the heart which we seek in silence.

The question remains: How, in a hectic day, with a family and two jobs, does one pray this prayer? Church tradition gives us many avenues, all of which are useful. To zero in on only one way, however, is to leave ourselves open to stagnation during times of dryness and desolation.

In the book, *The Way of a Pilgrim*,[3] a Russian peasant shares one such avenue, the Jesus Prayer. He shares the route he took in discovering the unceasing prayer of the heart. Instructed by a Russian monk, he begins to pray the Jesus Prayer: "Lord Jesus Christ, have mercy on me." He becomes so proficient in it, that he is soon saying that prayer several thousand times a day. One day, however, much to his amazement, he discovers that he no longer is saying the prayer with his lips, but with his heart. It had become a part of his very heartbeat. At that moment, we are told, the Russian peasant began to pray unceasingly.

Short prayers or Scripture phrases repeated over and over, give us an avenue for unceasing prayer. Any effort expended to incorporate this prayer into our lives will be worthwhile. Such a technique, however, is but one possible way to reach our goal.

In addition, our efforts to bring every aspect of our day into prayer, our efforts to bear the yoke of Jesus (i.e., the suffering of others), and our efforts to praise him with words and gestures and songs will help transform our hearts into the heart of Jesus. We do not complete such a journey overnight. It must continue through the boredom and routine of every day before results become apparent.

Throughout this endeavor, remember the importance of liturgy, especially Eucharist and reconciliation. A Catholic who prays in tongues every day, or says the rosary, or joins his/her heart to the Jesus Prayer, but does not seek food and nourishment through the sacraments, remains only partially fed.

Conclusion

Solitude, silence and unceasing prayer are critical if we are to maintain a life of discernment. Believe it or not, they help us remain sane and keep us rooted in reality in the midst of a society that is going mad and living in illusion. Solitude, silence and unceasing prayer will keep us from becoming so distracted by the agonies of these "last days" that we fall, together with those we are trying to save.

Finally, this desert spirituality re-models and re-minds us to be living witnesses of Jesus. Then, we will be living a life of discernment because we will be living the life of Jesus present in us.

Is it difficult? Yes, but less difficult than not beginning at all. Is it painful? Yes, but being stripped is always painful. Is it worth the effort? Absolutely, for there is no greater pearl, no greater treasure. Not to seek this is to value nothingness; to finally receive it, is to find Life itself.

We end this chapter as we began, with a story. There were three Desert Fathers. Every year they made a journey to visit Blessed Anthony—a holy and revered monk. During their times together, two of the Desert Fathers spoke with great relish and enthusiasm to Blessed Anthony. They shared insights, prayers, thoughts and dreams with their beloved monk. The third, however, remained silent throughout, never saying a word. After a long time, Blessed Anthony said to the silent monk, "You come here often to see me, but you never say a word; you never ask me anything." The monk replied, "Father Anthony, it is simply enough for me to see you."[4]

This is our goal: to let solitude, silence and unceasing prayer become so much a part of us, that people will not have to ask any questions; it will be enough for them to see us, because in us they will see Jesus.

---

[1] There are three classical writers to whom I am indebted: St. Ignatius of Loyola, St. John of the Cross, and St. Teresa of Avila. Two contemporary authors, without whom I would not have found this framework, are Thomas Merton and Henri Nouwen. I am particularly indebted to Nouwen's articles in *Sojourners*, later published in *The Way of the Heart: Desert Spirituality and Contemporary Ministry* (New York: Seabury Press, 1981), which gave me the categories of solitude, silence, and prayer.

[2] *The Sayings of the Desert Fathers*, translated by Benedicta Ward (London and Oxford: Mowbrays, 1975), 61.

[3] *The Way of a Pilgrim*, translated by R.M. French (New York: Seabury Press, 1970).

[4] *The Sayings of the Desert Fathers*, 6.

MEDITATION AND PRAYER

LIVES OF THE SAINTS VOL. I—A handy, popular, modern, beautifully illustrated "Lives of the Saints" with short, inspiring biographies for each day of the year. Large type. Over 70 illustrations. **Ask for No. 870**

LIVES OF THE SAINTS VOL. II—Companion volume to the best-selling "Lives of the Saints." It contains a new series of lives of saintly men and women for each day of the year—many of them newly canonized or beatified by the latest Popes. Large type. More than 60 illustrations.
Ask for No. 875

IMITATION OF CHRIST—By Thomas A Kempis. New edition. The one book that is second only to the Bible in popularity. This treasured book has brought peace to readers for many ages by showing how to follow the life of Christ to which all are called. Illustrated. **Ask for No. 320**

GIANT PRINT EDITION—This popular book offered in large, easy-to-read print. **Ask for No. 322**

INSPIRATIONAL THOUGHTS FOR EVERY DAY—By Rev. Thomas J. Donaghy. This book offers minute meditations for every day which contain a Scripture quotation, reflection, and prayer. **Ask for No. 194**

DAILY MEDITATION WITH SAINT AUGUSTINE—Compiled and edited by Rev. John Rotelle, O.S.A. Companion to the best-selling *Augustine Day by Day,* this book provides meditations and prayers for every day taken from the writings of Saint Augustine. **Ask for No. 176**

MINUTE MEDITATIONS FOR EACH DAY—By Rev. Bede Naegele, O.C.D. Short Scripture text, reflection, and prayer for each day that can be read in two minutes. 365 illustrations in color. **Ask for No. 190**

BIBLE DAY BY DAY—By Rev. John Kersten, S.V.D. Minute Bible meditations for every day including a short Scripture text and brief reflection. Printed in two colors with 300 illustrations. **Ask for No. 150**

WHEREVER CATHOLIC BOOKS ARE SOLD

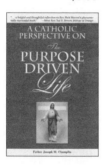

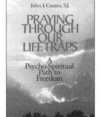

Additional Titles Published by Resurrection Press, a Catholic Book Publishing Imprint

A Rachel Rosary *Larry Kupferman*	$4.50
Advent of Understanding *Mary Gay Moore*	$5.95
Blessings All Around *Dolores Leckey*	$8.95
Catholic Is Wonderful *Mitch Finley*	$4.95
The Dilemma of Divorced Catholics *John T. Catoir, JCD*	$8.95
Edge of Greatness *Joni Woelfel*	$9.95
Feasts of Life *Jim Vlaun*	$12.95
Grace Notes *Lorraine Murray*	$9.95
Healing through the Mass *Robert DeGrandis, SSJ*	$9.95
Heart Peace *Adolfo Quezada*	$9.95
How Shall We Celebrate? *Lorraine Murray*	$6.95
How Shall We Pray? *James Gaffney*	$5.95
The Joy of Being an Altar Server *Joseph Champlin*	$5.95
The Joy of Being a Bereavement Minister *Nancy Stout*	$5.95
The Joy of Being a Catechist *Gloria Durka*	$4.95
The Joy of Being a Eucharistic Minister *Mitch Finley*	$5.95
The Joy of Being a Lector *Mitch Finley*	$5.95
The Joy of Being an Usher *Gretchen Hailer, RSHM*	$5.95
The Joy of Marriage Preparation *McDonough/Marinelli*	$5.95
The Joy of Music Ministry *J.M. Talbot*	$6.95
The Joy of Praying the Psalms *Nancy de Flon*	$5.95
The Joy of Praying the Rosary *James McNamara*	$5.95
The Joy of Preaching *Rod Damico*	$6.95
The Joy of Teaching *Joanmarie Smith*	$5.95
The Joy of Worshiping Together *Rod Damico*	$5.95
Lessons for Living from the 23rd Psalm *Victor Parachin*	$6.95
Lights in the Darkness *Ave Clark, O.P.*	$8.95
Loving Yourself for God's Sake *Adolfo Quezada*	$5.95
Magnetized by God *Robert E. Lauder*	$8.95
Meditations for Survivors of Suicide *Joni Woelfel*	$8.95
Mercy Flows *Rod Damico*	$9.95
Mother Teresa *Eugene Palumbo, S.D.B.*	$5.95
Mourning Sickness *Keith Smith*	$8.95
Our Grounds for Hope *Fulton J. Sheen*	$7.95
Personally Speaking *Jim Lisante*	$8.95
Power of One *Jim Lisante*	$9.95
Praying the Lord's Prayer with Mary *Muto/vanKaam*	$8.95
5-Minute Miracles *Linda Schubert*	$4.95
Sabbath Moments *Adolfo Quezada*	$6.95
Season of New Beginnings *Mitch Finley*	$4.95
Sometimes I Haven't Got a Prayer *Mary Sherry*	$8.95
St. Katharine Drexel *Daniel McSheffery*	$12.95
What He Did for Love *Francis X. Gaeta*	$5.95
Woman Soul *Pat Duffy, OP*	$7.95
You Are My Beloved *Mitch Finley*	$10.95

For a free catalog call 1-800-892-6657
www.catholicbookpublishing.com